Choice with Equity

The Hoover Institution gratefully acknowledges the following individuals and foundations for their significant support of the

Initiative
on
American Public Education

KORET FOUNDATION
TAD AND DIANNE TAUBE
LYNDE AND HARRY BRADLEY FOUNDATION
BOYD AND JILL SMITH
JACK AND MARY LOIS WHEATLEY
FRANKLIN AND CATHERINE JOHNSON
JERRY AND PATTI HUME
DORIS AND DONALD FISHER
BERNARD LEE SCHWARTZ FOUNDATION

The Hoover Institution gratefully acknowledges generous support from

TAD AND DIANNE TAUBE
TAUBE FAMILY FOUNDATION
KORET FOUNDATION

Founders of the program on American Institutions and Economic Performance

and Cornerstone gifts from

SARAH SCAIFE FOUNDATION

Choice with Equity

EDITED BY
Paul T. Hill

CONTRIBUTING AUTHORS
David E. Campbell
John E. Chubb
Kacey Guin
Eric A. Hanushek
Paul T. Hill
Caroline M. Hoxby
Terry M. Moe
Paul E. Peterson
Martin R. West

HOOVER INSTITUTION PRESS
STANFORD UNIVERSITY   STANFORD, CALIFORNIA

www.hoover.org

Hoover Institution Press Publication No. 513

First printing 2002
07 06 05 04 03 02   9 8 7 6 5 4 3 2 1

Manufactured in the United States of America

The paper used in this publication meets the minimum requirements of the American National Standard for Information Sciences— Permanence of Paper for Printed Library Materials, ANSI Z39.48–1984.

Library of Congress Cataloging-in-Publication Data
Choice with equity / edited by Paul T. Hill
    p. cm. — (Hoover Institution Press publication; no. 513)
"An assessment by the Koret Task Force on K–12 Education"—Cover.
Includes bibliographical references and index.
    ISBN 0-8179-3891-5 (alk.paper) — ISBN 0-8179-3892-3 (alk. paper)
    1. School choice—Social aspects—United States. 2. Educational equal-ization—United States. I. Hill, Paul Thomas, 1943– II. Koret Task Force on K–12 education. III. Hoover Institution Press publication; 513.
 LB1027.9 .C53 2002
 379.1'11—dc21
                                         2002003152

Contents

Foreword

The Koret Task Force on K–12 Education—a joint endeavor of the Koret Foundation of San Francisco and the Hoover Institution—is a group of eleven education policy experts that seeks to evaluate the existing evidence on school reform measures and to conduct research on the quality and productivity of K–12 education in the United States. Immediately after the task force formally convened in 1999, its investment in research and writing began.

This venture is the conception of joint thinking between Tad Taube, president of the Koret Foundation, and myself. The Koret Foundation is a philanthropic organization that has decided to focus heavily on education issues in the United States. We both felt strongly that the Hoover Institution could contribute to the national dialogue on how to improve American public education. Thus, the Hoover Institution, with significant support from the Koret Foundation, embarked on a multiyear effort to identify and convey factual information about the state of American education, as well as to generate ideas that would enhance the opportunity for all children to gain more knowledge and assemble better skills.

The first book released by the Koret Task Force and edited by task force member Terry M. Moe, *A Primer on America's Schools* (Hoover Institution Press, 2001), cuts through the complexities and often unwarranted assumptions in the education debate and conveys essential information pertaining to this important public policy issue. In *A Primer on America's Schools*, this group takes an important step toward school reform by providing a broad overview of the current state of American education.

The *Primer* provided the foundation for the task force to proceed with two new projects on the important issues of school choice and accountability. These books are fresh contributions to a field that has become frozen by ideological disputes, bureaucratic resistance, and establishment views.

In *Choice with Equity*, edited by task force member Paul T. Hill, six members of the task force take a hard look at the possible downsides of choice in education. These scholars ask whether choice is likely to increase student segregation by race and class or to harm students whose parents are not the first to choose a school. They acknowledge the risks inherent in poorly designed choice programs and suggest how choice can be structured to protect and actually benefit the disadvantaged.

In *School Accountability*, edited by task force members Williamson M. Evers and Herbert J. Walberg, scholars describe the present state of school accountability, how it evolved, how it succeeded and failed, and how it can best be improved. This book describes the range of efforts and identifies the best principles and practices that will improve accountability and hence our nation's schools.

I thank the task force members responsible for the design of these volumes and the editors and authors who contributed to them. I also thank the Koret Foundation for the continuing generous financial support to sustain the work of the task force, especially Tad Taube for his help in creating the intellectual foundation for the task force and the Hoover Institution's Initiative on American Public Education.

The Koret Task Force on K–12 Education forms the centerpiece of the Hoover Institution's Initiative on American Public Education, with the overall goal of presenting pertinent facts surrounding the current debate, contributing to the debate as a constructive commentator, and generating new ideas relating to education reform. This is a multiyear commitment to the production of research and writing on education reform that citizens of the United States should be considering as a matter of public policy. We could not have launched this ambitious initiative without the help of the many individuals who have stepped forward to support this effort, many of whom are explicitly mentioned on the acknowledgment page.

John Raisian
Director
Hoover Institution

1

Introduction

Paul T. Hill

An observer from another planet might think our national debate about school choice is a ritual. One group offers a litany of evidence and arguments about the benefits of choice, and another group responds ritualistically with claims about the harm choice can do. Neither side seriously confronts the arguments of the other, and the debate does not change. But of course the visitor would miss the point. The debate is serious, and members of at least one side, those in favor of greater choice for families and educators, intend for it to go somewhere. The opponents of choice, knowing that stalemate favors their side, might be content to protract the debate indefinitely. But they, too, take the debate seriously and think important matters are at stake.

The proponents of K–12 school choice focus on its possible benefits: Children could be placed in schools that match their interests and approaches to learning, and might therefore learn more deeply and efficiently; families and school staffs that could choose each other might develop relationships of trust and confidence; schools needing to compete for students and teachers might develop focused and consistent approaches to instruction.[1]

Opponents are skeptical about choice's possible benefits, but their arguments focus elsewhere, on the harm choice might do. The most alert and aggressive families might take all the spaces in the best schools, and schools might make themselves look effective by only admitting the children of intact middle-class homes. Schools left behind after the advantaged depart might be weakened as educational institutions; and the children in those schools, disproportionate numbers of whom would be from low-income and minority families, would receive worse instruction after choice than before.[2]

"Choice" can mean many things—from allowing parents to choose among a limited group of existing public schools to giving parents public vouchers that they can redeem for tuition in any private school. Choice programs differ on two dimensions: (1) who provides schools, and (2) who decides what school a particular child will attend. The base non-choice case is the traditional school district, which is a monopoly provider of all publicly funded schools in a locality, and assigns children to schools, usually on the basis of residence. The extreme choice case is the pure voucher system in which government pays for schooling but does nothing to provide it. A less extreme case is regulated vouchers, in which government licenses schools, provides information about all schools, and manages fair admissions lotteries. "Public school choice" is another variant: it preserves the school district monopoly but allows families to choose which

---

[1]These are not all the benefits claimed by choice proponents, but most others are derived from these. For example, choice supporters claim that competition would force regular public schools to improve. This claim is based on the more fundamental assumed benefit that entrepreneurial schools will compete with regular public schools on the basis of instructional quality.

[2]These are not all the harms of choice cited by opponents, but most others are derived from these. For example, choice opponents claim that choice will deprive low-income children of the benefits of association with students from middle-class families. This claim is based on the more fundamental assumption that choice will lead to increased segregation.

schools their children will attend. Finally, chartering and school contracting allow parents to choose among publicly funded schools, which are provided by independent groups under contract with government agencies.

Different forms of choice inspire hope and fear in different degrees. Public school choice inspires neither fear nor hope: it is unlikely either to change the kinds of schools made available or to give parents many real options. Any other form of choice, even charter schools, inspires fears, for example, that school providers and better-off families will monopolize information and use it to their own advantage; or the fear that there will always be only a few good schools, so that schools, not families, will be the real choosers and the best schools will choose the easiest to educate. Opponents also fear that independently run schools (whether charters or wholly independent schools under a voucher scheme) will compete on the basis of whom they exclude.

Each side works to develop evidence buttressing its case. Thus, proponents of choice show that choice leads to gains in student learning, especially for minority and disadvantaged children, and opponents show that families of particular income levels or ethnicities cluster in schools of choice. Neither side's evidence resolves the debate. First, the results, good and bad, are never overwhelming. Even under the best-controlled quasi-experimental programs studied by Peterson and his colleagues, students who attend schools of choice do not always learn at a dramatically higher rate than similar students who remain in regular public schools. Moreover, when compared with regular public schools, choice programs often do not segregate students or create larger gaps in achievement between ethnic and income groups. A second reason for the lack of a clear answer to the debate is that neither side can marshal compelling evidence to "convert" people—even intellectually honest people amenable to evidence—on the other side. People on both sides can dismiss the other's evidence as weak, debatable, or highly dependent on special characteristics of the circumstances under which it was obtained.

But of course serious debaters care less about converting opponents than persuading the audience. Both sides hope to persuade educators, parents, voters, and public officials that choice can (alternatively) lead to overall improvements in student learning or to worse schools and less learning for the disadvantaged. Though neither side has been completely successful, here the proponents of choice have an advantage. Many laypersons know children who benefited when their parents put them in a parochial school or campaigned successfully for a change in public school placement. Many laypersons are also unimpressed by the regular public schools' track records on racial and class integration and effective education of the disadvantaged. These groups—especially, according to many polls, African American parents in big cities—are open to evidence about the benefits of choice and are not particularly concerned about its harms.

There are, however, constituencies that are hard to persuade about the benefits of choice, and easy to persuade about its risks. In addition to unionized public school teachers and other school district employees, all of whom would experience new demands and changes in their jobs, other groups are more inclined to worry about the harm that choice might do. These include liberals whose aspirations for public education focus on racial integration more than any other outcome, individuals convinced that regular public schools were their own route into society's mainstream, and parents of children whom the existing public schools are serving well.

Our national debate about choice will not be resolved by one side's finally finding that one bit of evidence that vanquishes the other. Resolution will come only when large numbers of laypersons, parents, educators, and elected officials come to believe one of four things:

• That the potential benefits of choice are so great that they outweigh any possible risks; or

• The risks of choice can be so well controlled that it is worthwhile even if benefits are moderate; or

• The risks of choice, though moderate, still outweigh its potential benefits; or

• The risks of choice are so great that no benefit can possibly offset them.

From where we are today it could take some time for the debate over choice to arrive at any of these endpoints. But there is a real cost to protracted debate. If choice can lead to better schools and smaller achievement gaps between rich and poor or white and minority children, these benefits should not be postponed. Humans are schoolchildren only once in their lives, and learning opportunities delayed are learning opportunities denied. On the other hand, if the risks of choice are truly so great as to outweigh its benefits, no one should be encouraged to rely on efforts to use it as a way of providing better schools.

MOVING THE DEBATE

This book is an attempt to move the debate on choice ahead by focusing on the risks of choice and how they can be controlled. It is a product of the Koret Task Force, an interdisciplinary group of scholars convened by the Hoover Institution to apply the highest standards of social science research to education policy. The authors of this book, all easily identified as members of the pro-choice side, have written a fair amount of the literature on the benefits of choice. We have, however, long understood that benefits are only one side of the ledger. All of us have tried to acknowledge and take account of the risks, though that has never been our main focus. All of us understand that programs of school choice could, if poorly designed or perversely implemented, have negative consequences.

We undertook this book because we know that America cannot afford to slip back toward a dual school system in which children are separated by race or in which some children get the best of everything and others do not learn enough to enter college or get good jobs. We know that there are not enough good schools for all the children in this country, and that the shortage is especially severe in the central neighborhoods of big cities. We also know that all Americans, not just a few, need to be taught to value mutual respect, freedom of speech, and open democratic decision-making. As citizens and as parents we would not support choice or any other policy that would deny poor and minority children a good education, reduce the numbers of good schools, or weaken our country's capacity for civil discourse.

In acknowledging the importance of these issues, we do not endorse the ways they have been approached by opponents of choice. Though respectable scholars have claimed to document the harms of choice, most have artfully cited situations in which the harms are poorly defined, choice is poorly implemented, or its effects are confounded with those of other factors. Thus, for example, arguing that choice will create segregation, Bruce Fuller, Richard Elmore, and Gary Orfield claim that the "cultural logic of families" will lead parents to choose schools that serve only people who have similar beliefs.[3] However, similarity is loosely defined to include even the very specific belief that a given school is the right one for a particular child. Thus, a term originally coined by these authors to cover religious and political beliefs is stretched to cover simple preferences for a school. By that stretch the authors are able to claim to show that choice will allow families to choose segregated schools.[4]

Based on experience in New Zealand, Ted Fiske and Helen Ladd speculate that choice leads to worse education

---

[3]Bruce Fuller, Richard F. Elmore, and Gary Orfield, "Policy-Making in the Dark: Illuminating the School Choice Debate," in Bruce Fuller, Richard F. Elmore, and Gary Orfield, eds., *Who Chooses? Who Loses? Culture, Institutions, and the Unequal Effects of School Choice* (New York: Teachers College Press, 1996), pp. 1–24.

[4]For a similar argument see Amy Stuart Wells, Alejandra Scott, Janelle Holme, and Jennifer Jellison, "Charter Schools as Postmodern Paradox: Rethinking Social Stratification in an Age of Deregulated School Choice," *Harvard Education Review* 69, no. 2 (Summer 1999): 172–204.

for low-income children.[5] Though they have no data on student performance, they draw this conclusion from the fact that some schools got dramatically worse on measures of instructional resource quality. Yet they ignore the fact that total enrollments in highly regarded schools grew, and enrollments in lesser schools shrank, dramatically. They also ignore some program design elements that led to creation of have- and have-not schools: New Zealand's program continued civil service employment of teachers and charged schools the same amount for every teacher they employed, regardless of what a teacher was actually paid. This allowed the most popular schools to hire all the highest-paid and best-regarded teachers, and left the least popular schools with only the least experienced or most lowly regarded teachers. New Zealand also did not close failing schools, nor did it allow the formation of new schools, and it let popular schools grow to any size they pleased. Taken together, these factors—not choice itself—caused the harmful outcomes reported.

Amy Stuart Wells, in a contribution to the Fuller, Elmore, Orfield volume based on a survey of urban African American students who took an opportunity to enroll in suburban schools, observes that minority choosers are interested in having contacts with whites and are critical of all-black schools.[6] She concludes that choosers were eager to escape other blacks and not interested in school quality. Observing that students who did not choose were those who feared the competition they might encounter in white or higher-status schools, she argues that non-choosers would be left behind "in an educational free market predicated on the existence of both winners and losers." Thus, according to Wells, though choosers do not select better schooling, non-choosers are condemned to staying in the worst schools.

---

[5]Ted Fiske and Helen F. Ladd, *When Schools Compete: A Cautionary Tale* (Washington, D.C.: Brookings Institution Press, 2000).

[6]Amy Stuart Wells, "African American Students' View of School Choice," in Fuller, Elmore, and Orfield, eds., *Who Chooses? Who Loses?* pp. 25–49.

The fact that these analyses are weak and one-sided does not mean that choice can do no harm. To the contrary, like any powerful tool it can do harm as well as good. As Terry Moe's recent book on Americans' views of choice shows, there are parents who would use choice to escape from others and to cluster in privileged enclaves.[7] As some have argued based on other countries' experience, schools with no constraints on whom they admit can also succumb to the temptation to admit only the easiest to educate and the most congenial.[8] The authors of this book are not neutral about such potential consequences of choice: we are against them.

Moreover, as people who think choice can lead to better education for the children whom our schools now serve least well, we are not complacent about issues of design and implementation. We are against leaving equity and quality in education to chance, no matter how schools are run or who decides what schools children will attend. For that reason each of us has been critical of the predominant model of public education, which relies on bureaucratic process to run schools and allocate opportunities. We have condemned school districts for their rank carelessness in allowing the most advantaged children to get the best teachers and condemning the neediest children to the weakest teachers and most turbulent schools. No matter how optimistic we are about choice we cannot take an indulgent approach to it and a critical approach to the current public education system.

To date, however, the opponents of choice have succeeded in assigning the entire burden of proof to choice supporters. Show us, they say, that choice will not favor the alert and ag-

---

[7]Terry M. Moe, *Schools, Vouchers, and the American Public* (Washington, D.C.: Brookings Institution Press, 2001), esp. chap. 5, "The Attraction of Private Schools."

[8]See, e.g., Martin Carnoy, "National Voucher Plans in Chile and Sweden: Did Privatization Reforms Make for Better Education?" *Comparative Education Review* 42, no. 3 (August 1998): p. 307. See also Gregory Walford, ed., "School Choice and the Quasi-market," *Oxford Studies in Comparative Education* 6, no. 1 (1996).

gressive and disfavor those who do not know how to recognize good schools or cannot organize themselves to campaign for admission. The authors of this book accept some, but not all, of this burden of proof. The part we accept is the responsibility to provide hard data whose provenance is clear, and to compare situations that are identical except for the presence or absence of choice. But we reject as biased any requirement that choice be shown never to create advantages for anyone, and never to allow people of like mind to join with one another.

Of course choice creates opportunities that some people take advantage of. But, as Paul Hill and Kacey Guin demonstrate in Chapter 2, so does every other way of organizing schooling, including the bureaucratic methods now used to provide public education. They show that existing public school districts allow a great deal of racial segregation. Moreover, in the absence of transparent choice mechanisms, more sophisticated parents manipulate bureaucratic processes to their advantage. The result is that middle-class, often white, children monopolize the best programs and teachers the public school system has to offer. Hill and Guin conclude that the results of choice programs need to be compared against a baseline of the public school system's real performance, not to its lofty aspirations or to ideal standards that no practical arrangement can meet.

Using that standard of comparison this book looks hard at two ways that choice might do harm, not good, from the perspectives of educational equity and quality. The first is that choice might exacerbate segregation of students by race or income. This would violate the constitutional principles established by *Brown v. Board of Education*; worse, it would probably imply that children of different races and income groups would be educated in different ways and to different standards. The second potential harm we examine is a decline in the quality of regular neighborhood public schools, which could harm children left behind in those schools even as children whose families were quick to choose benefited.

We focus on these two potential harms of choice because most other objections stem from them. For example, some fear that choice might lead to a balkanization of society resulting from differences in children's educational experiences. That claim goes beyond the segregation argument, to assert (counter to American experiences with graduates of parochial schools) that people from different educational backgrounds cannot engage in democratic discourse. But the claim starts with the assertion that choice will lead to the sorting of children by race, sex, religion, and other characteristics. If this does not happen, the "balkanization" argument loses its main premise.

Chapters 3 and 4 address the segregation issue from the point of view of real-world choice programs. In Chapter 3, Paul E. Peterson, David E. Campbell, and Martin R. West compare the characteristics of applicants to a national privately funded voucher system, the national Children's Scholarship Fund, with the characteristics of a national sample of the eligible population. They also compare those who use the vouchers with those who were offered vouchers but did not use them. They find that voucher applicants are in general modestly advantaged relative to eligible nonapplicants, although African Americans are especially likely to apply. The main factor driving voucher applicants appears to be dissatisfaction with the public school that a family's children attend. Among families that are offered vouchers, the families most likely to use them are Catholic. Families in communities with large numbers of private schools are also more likely to use a voucher if it is offered. Peterson and his colleagues find no evidence that this voucher program has contributed to racial segregation in the public schools. To the contrary, by helping poor and minority students attend private schools, the Children's Scholarship Fund has increased the numbers of minority and economically disadvantaged students in public schools and has also increased their numbers in private schools.

In Chapter 4, John E. Chubb provides new evidence on the question of whether privately run schools receiving public funds are likely to promote segregation by handpicking white or economically advantaged children. He draws on the experience of Edison, a private company that manages schools under contract with local public authorities. His data on school enrollment show that Edison schools on average draw a student population that is poorer and more heavily African American than the school districts in which they are located. This reflects Edison's corporate strategy, which is to demonstrate that its schools can work for all students. It also reflects local authorities' motives in hiring Edison, often to serve neighborhoods where conventional public schools have not performed well. Chubb's data do not prove that all schools operating under choice schemes would serve such a diverse population, but they do show that critics are wrong when they say that schools of choice inevitably create privileged enclaves.

Chapters 5 and 6 address the issue of harm to schools left behind by the first families to take advantage of new options. In Chapter 5, Eric A. Hanushek asks whether choice will harm the children whose parents are slowest to take advantage of new options. Some critics fear that when choice is introduced, the "students left behind" will suffer because their peers will be poorer, less motivated, and more heavily minority than before. Reviewing research on the ways the characteristics of a student's classmates affect his or her academic performance, Hanushek concludes that the evidence is mixed. Though a student's own family income and academic ability are highly correlated with achievement, going to school with advantaged peers adds little. However, racial composition can matter: students who attend schools that are heavily African American learn less than would be predicted from their family income and academic ability. Moreover, as Hanushek concludes, school racial and income composition can have indirect effects. Three correlates of student poverty and minority status—high student mobility, capable teachers' avoidance of schools in troubled neighborhoods, and inequitable allocation of funds within school districts—can prevent delivery of a coherent instructional program.

In Chapter 6, Caroline M. Hoxby asks whether the competition for students that choice engenders can help or harm public schools. Does choice create a zero-sum game in which the existing public schools get weaker as alternatives develop? Or might competition lead to stronger schools all around, including conventional public schools that have developed better instructional methods and more coherent instructional programs? Using results from Milwaukee, Hoxby shows that public schools facing the most severe competition raised student test scores much more than schools facing little or no competition. Similarly, Michigan and Arizona schools facing the most severe competition from charter schools raised test scores more than schools facing less competition. In both states, rapid improvement began immediately after the public schools first felt competition from charter schools. These gains were particularly dramatic for African American and Hispanic students in schools facing competition. Improving schools took sensible actions that did not involve massive new funding or changes in the student body: they focused time and attention on instruction, unified the work of teachers, and tried to replace teachers who would not cooperate with the improvement program.

In Chapter 7, Terry M. Moe reviews the potential harms of choice and shows how program design can help avoid—or exacerbate—them. Many decisions have to be made about program structure, and these determine, for example, whether poor and minority students have equitable access to good schools, or whether wealthy parents will use their own money to distort the distribution of good teachers and instructional programs. Moe argues that no one seriously suggests that choice should be a free-for-all without rules and structure. Like our free economy, an educational system based on choice would need rules to ensure that schools make honest claims, that all choosers have information, and that no one can monopolize all the best resources. Creating fair rules of the game is a great challenge to our political system—one that it has failed to meet in the design and operation of public school districts. Moe concludes that choice schemes can be designed to be equitable and to create pressures for constant school improvement. But this cannot be done unless Americans recognize the possible risks and choose structures that address them.

Taken together, the chapters in this book show a way out of our ritualized debates about choice. People who favor choice and those who fear it can agree that choice alone does not cause any outcome, good or bad; it provides a mechanism whereby families seek what they consider the best schools for their children, and it can lead to segregation. But choice can also lead to fairer allocations of opportunities and less segregation than now exists. Everything depends on how choice is structured and managed. Choice can support the development of better schools and fairer allocation of the most desirable opportunities. Whether choice benefits children as much as it can—or whether it does little to help those most in need—depends upon how we Americans decide to govern it.

2

Baselines for Assessment of Choice Programs[*]

Paul T. Hill with Kacey Guin

Critics of choice argue that it will allow alert and aggressive parents to get the best of everything for their children, leaving poor and minority children concentrated in the worst schools.[1] But choice is not the only mechanism whereby this occurs. Alert and aggressive parents work the bureaucracy to get the best for their children. Thus, choice programs should be compared against the real performance of the current public education system, not its idealized aspirations.

The purpose of this chapter is to establish an appropriate baseline against which choice programs can be assessed. How far does the current system of bureaucratic allocation diverge from its aspirations to equal opportunity for all? Under the current system, how much are students sorted by race and class, and how unevenly allocated are the best and worst educational experiences? The answers to these questions are important for two reasons:

---

[*]We are grateful to Jacob Adams for an especially demanding and constructive review of an earlier draft.

[1]Throughout this chapter we use the term "critics of choice" to refer to scholars and analysts who fear that choice will harm the interests of the poor and disadvantaged. These critics include: B. Fuller, "School Choice: Who Gains,

1. They establish defensible baselines against which choice programs can be compared. If the current ways of allocating educational opportunities lead to inequality by race, class, or income, then choice programs should not be assessed against the ideal. Instead, their results should be compared with the actual performance of the existing system.

2. They establish criteria for the design of choice programs. Whether or not choice programs are on average no worse than other ways of allocating educational programs, there are still ethical and public policy reasons for designing and operating choice schemes to minimize sorting and equalize access to the best schools and teachers. Programs so designed can produce greater equity in two ways: first, through fair allocation, and second, by increasing the demand for better options and thus ultimately stimulating the supply.[2]

Who Loses?" *Issues in Science and Technology* 12, no. 3 (1996): 61–67; and B. Fuller, "Is School Choice Working?" *Educational Leadership* 54, no. 2 (1996): 37–40 (concludes that choice may worsen racial separation in schools); K. B. Smith and K. J. Meier, "School Choice: Panacea or Pandora's Box?" *Phi Delta Kappan* 77, no. 4 (1995): 312 (concludes that families choose schools in order to associate with others of the same religion and to avoid racial minorities); R. F. Elmore and B. Fuller, "Empirical Research on Education Choice: What Are the Implications for Policy-Makers?" in B. Fuller, R. F. Elmore, and G. Orfield, eds., *Who Chooses? Who Loses?* (New York: Teachers College Press, 1996) ("Increasing educational choice is likely to increase separation of students by race, social class, and cultural background," p. 189. Elmore et al. argue that regardless of the choice program design, the differences in choosers and non-choosers are such that choice programs will contribute to social stratification, not greater equality); A. S. Wells, "Charter School Reform in California: Does It Meet Expectations?" *Phi Delta Kappan* 8, no. 4 (1998): 305–12 (argues that charter schools will worsen inequality); M. Schneider, M. Marschall, P. Teske, and C. Roch, "School Choice and Culture Wars in the Classroom: What Different Parents Seek from Education," *Social Science Quarterly* 79, no. 3 (1998): 489–501 (argues that school choice will increase segregation because parents of different ethnicities and SES status have fundamental differences in their expectations of education for their children).

[2]See Paul T. Hill, "The Supply Side of Choice," in Frank Kemmerer and Stephen Sugarman, *School Choice and Social Controversy* (Washington, D.C.: Brookings Institution Press, 2000).

Bureaucratic modes of decision-making do not eliminate self-seeking—they only make it covert. When the supply of desirable schools, programs, or teachers is limited the most aggressive get the best and, by implication, deprive others. In bureaucracies, the advantage goes to people who have contacts, understand how the game is played, can talk the language of key administrators, can write letters and threaten appeals, and have the time and determination to persist. These attributes have a strong class bias. As a result, bureaucratic decision-making can create segregation of students and uneven distribution of benefits. These, of course, are the very outcomes that people fear choice will produce.

Choice is another mechanism by which people seek the best for themselves and their children. The most knowledgeable are first to identify the best opportunities, and the most aggressive are the ones most likely to sign up early, know how to get the most advantageous place in a lottery, and be able to impress the people (for example, admissions officers) who can pick from among many applicants.

Self-seeking would not matter if all schools, teachers, or courses were equally good. But that is not the case. To the contrary, some schools are much better than others, even when quality is measured fairly on the basis of what they add to their students' knowledge.[3] There is also reason to believe that some teachers are much better than others[4] and also that some courses of study are much more likely to prepare students for jobs and higher education than others.[5] Because some students thrive in schools that would not be good for other students, there is more than one way to rank quality. But however quality is defined, the "best"

---

[3]See Fred M. Newmann, Bets Ann Smith, Elaine Allensworth, and Anthony S. Bryk, *School Instructional Program Coherence: Benefits and Challenges* (Chicago: Consortium on Chicago School Research, 2000).

[4]Kati Haycock et al., *Achievement in America 2000* (Washington, D.C.: Education Trust, 2000).

[5]See, e.g., Heather Rose and Julian R. Betts, *Math Matters: The Links Between High School Curriculum, College Graduation, and Earnings* (San Francisco: Public Policy Institute of California, 2001).

schools and teachers are usually in short supply. That is why the most respected private schools have long waiting lists and why parents camp out in parking lots to register their children in public magnet schools.

Some public school districts try to provide a quality school for every student, but they are thwarted by scarcity. There are only so many experienced teachers, only so many principals who can create a positive school climate, and only so many people who both understand science and mathematics and want to teach those subjects. Schools are like any other enterprise that depends on people. Only so many children can take chemistry from the fabled teacher whose students regularly end up in medical school. Someone will get the burned-out old teacher in his last year, or the brand new teacher whose command of subject matter and classroom management skills is shaky. Some schools or districts might maximize the average quality of their staffs, encourage the burned-out to retire earlier, or do a better job of mentoring inexperienced teachers. But there will always be differences in quality, both real and perceived.

Scarcity begets competition. Though some parents will knowingly accept less than the best for their children, many will not. Among those who try to get the best (or to spare their children contact with the worst), some will fare better than others. Those who do not try to compete will probably do worse than even the least successful competitors.[6]

How people compete for schools and teachers depends on the way opportunities are allocated. When parents are free to apply to any public school, the most competitive study the options, apply early, and try to make sure they apply to some desirable schools where the probability of admission is high. When parents are assigned to schools, the most competitive learn who are the best and worst teachers and programs and campaign to get these for their

[6]Abby Goodnough, "How to Get Your Child the Right Teacher Next Fall," *New York Times Magazine,* May 13, 2001.

children.[7] The rules of competition inevitably allocate advantages and disadvantages. When the rules allow exceptions to mandatory school assignment, the most competitive families learn how decisions are made and frame their transfer appeals in the appropriate terms. The most competitive also figure out who makes the final decision on transfer requests, and seek ways to get special consideration.

Thus, choice is only one way of allocating educational opportunities. Self-seeking and competition are universal. Only the means differ. The advantage of choice is that advantage seeking is transparent: its effects can be readily observed, and it can be designed out (for example, by admissions lotteries). In bureaucracies, self-seeking is covert, and therefore harder to observe and remedy.

Whether choice or bureaucratic decision-making leads to a "fairer" allocation of opportunities is an empirical question. Under both systems, the advantaged are likely to get a disproportionate share of the best and the disadvantaged are likely to get the worst. Thus the question for public debate is not whether choice leads to inequalities but whether it leads to any greater inequalities than does non-choice.

Perhaps a better way to formulate this question is whether overt choice leads to the same or lesser inequities than does covert choice. As David Menefee-Libey of Pomona College has suggested, someone always exercises choices, even in bureaucratic systems. What matters is whether everyone or just some people have choices, and whether choices are made openly or in secret. Overt school choice occurs when everyone can choose and everyone who picks a particular school has an equal chance of getting in. Covert choice occurs when there are no structured mechanisms for expressing choices and allocating opportunities, so that families who want particular options are forced to campaign for them. Because families must go out of their way to express choices, and

---

[7]See Alfie Kohn, "Only for My Kid: How Privileged Parents Undermine School Reform," *Phi Delta Kappan* (April 1998): 569–77.

must work the bureaucracy to get what they want, covert choice strongly favors the sophisticated and well placed.

Critics of overt education choice proposals assert that they make matters worse for the disadvantaged and promote development of privileged enclaves for the advantaged. The implication of these statements is that choice makes things worse than they are now. But the evidence provided is often quite different. It shows that overt choice leads to some unequal outcomes, not that choice leads to more unequal outcomes than are attained by the covert choice system that now prevails.

ESTABLISHING A BASELINE

Critics claim that choice will worsen segregation and other forms of inequity. This chapter asks, compared with what? The proper baseline against which to assess the effects of choice is the performance of the current system, not some idealized system in which no differences exist. As Stephen Gorard and his colleagues observe about universal choice in Britain, "The stratifying effect of market forces in schools depends, to large extent, on the *status ante*. What we have shown is not that choice is SES-free but that it is certainly no worse, and probably a great deal better, than simply assigning children to their nearest school to be educated with similar children living in similar housing conditions."[8]

Using the current system's performance as a baseline for comparison does not imply satisfaction with things as they are. Programs that rely on choice should (and, as Terry Moe's final chapter in this volume suggests, can) be designed to produce less segregation and more equitable distributions of resources and opportunity than now exist. This chapter, however, focuses narrowly on whether defenders of the current system are justified in opposing choice on grounds that it inevitably worsens segregation and inequitable distribution of resources. Our narrow question is this: If public funds were

---

[8]S. Gorard, J. Fitz, and C. Taylor, "School Choice Impacts: What Do We Know?" *Educational Researcher* 30, no. 7 (October 2001): 22.

used to create many options for families, and families were free to choose among those options, would segregation and inequity be worse than they are now?

In order to understand the practical consequences of choice proposals we must ignore choices that would exist under any and all circumstances. "Choice" covers a wide range of situations. Theoretically, every parent is free under the Constitution to choose to send a child to a tuition-charging private school, or to move away from a state or locality whose schools they consider inadequate, or even to tutor a child at home. It is important to distinguish between choices that families have if they are willing to pay for education themselves or move their residence—constitutionally guaranteed choice—and the choices that families face if they want the government to pay for education and they do not want to (or cannot) move—which we shall call policy-determined choice. Constitutionally guaranteed choices exist regardless of what government does. Policy-determined choices depend on the rules government sets.

Our goal in this chapter is to understand the effects of changes in government policy: we ask, would government action to expand choice lead to greater inequalities than now exist under the current policies concerning government financing and student assignment to schools? In this chapter we therefore focus on policy-determined choice.

Figure 1 illustrates the difference between constitutional choice and the many forms of policy-determined choice. Government can set supply-side rules, saying who can operate schools and receive government funds. Government can also set demand-side rules, saying which families are free to choose among government-funded schools, and which of all available schools they may choose. In Figure 1, under policy-determined choice, different supply-side arrangements are defined by the rows and demand-side arrangements by the columns. Every intersection of a row with a column defines a specific choice policy. Some of the cells are shaded because they imply contradictions between supply- and demand-side policies.

Constitutionally guaranteed choice	Policy-determined choice				
• Paying private school tuition • Moving across jurisdictions • Home schooling	District-operated schools	Limited choice	Controlled choice Reinventing choice	Regulated vouchers	Unregulated vouchers
	Chartered schools				
	Independently run schools				
	Coursework offered by many providers				
		Only certain families choose	All families choose among district-designated schools	All families choose among licensed schools	All families choose any provider

FIGURE 1.   Forms of Choice in K–12 Education

As Figure 1 illustrates on the supply side, policy could provide that government will fund only schools operated by school districts. Or government could fund charter schools, operating under contract with school districts or other government agencies. Or policy could provide that government will fund any independently run school that families choose. Finally, government could pay for instructional programs that are narrower than whole schools—paying if a child took English from one organization, math from another, and Spanish from yet another.

On the demand side, policy could provide that only certain families (for example, the poor) may choose. Or that every family may choose among several schools, but still limit choices on the basis of neighborhood, racial balance, or other factors. Or policy may say that families may choose absolutely any school that is licensed. Finally, policy could say that families may choose absolutely any provider, whether licensed or not.

Figure 1 contains five fields that define the different kinds of policy-determined choice. Some of the fields cover only one cell; others cover more than one. For example, the combination of any supply-side rule with "only certain families may choose" is called "limited choice." "Controlled choice" means that policy limits either what schools may be chosen or who may choose. "Reinventing choice" identifies the types of choice created when school districts charter or contract with independent groups to run schools. "Regulated vouchers" refers to the voucher scheme proposed by John Chubb and Terry Moe, which allows any group to run schools but requires all to be licensed.[9] "Unregulated vouchers" refers to Milton and Rose Friedman's scheme, which allows parents to purchase any form of education they consider appropriate.[10]

In this chapter we take the sorting effects of constitutional choice as a given and focus on the consequences of choices among publicly funded schools within a single school district. We compare the effects of choice programs against the sorting that occurs within public school systems where the bureaucracy determines what schools children will attend. Any such comparison might be slightly biased against choice programs. As Hoxby and others have argued, freedom of choice on both the supply and demand sides will improve the supply of schools in a locality, and might reduce the rates at which advantaged families depart for other districts, or home school, or pay for private education.[11] In a district where competition produced a variety of academically excellent schools, families might choose on the basis of instructional methods rather than on student body composition or perceived quality of student life. This might lead to far less segregation and inequity than prevails in the current system. In this analysis,

[9]J. Chubb and T. Moe, *Politics, Markets, and America's Schools* (Washington, D.C.: Brookings Institution Press, 1990).

[10]Milton and Rose Friedman, *Free to Choose: A Personal Statement* (New York: Harcourt Brace Jovanovich, 1980).

[11]See C. Hoxby, "Does Competition Among Public Schools Benefit Students and Taxpayers?" *American Economic Review* 90, no. 5 (2000): 1209–38.

however, our interest is in the current system, not in all possible scenarios in which choice might have positive consequences.

We provide a baseline of evidence by which the consequences of choice can be compared with the results of the current public school system. Some critics of choice would like to compare it against an idealized form of the current system: Gary Orfield, among others, asserts that the current system can be perfected to eliminate any form of segregation, even that based on residential choices. He argues for "deny[ing privileged families] the possibility of finding nearby all-white schools," via creation of metropolitan-wide school districts, and massive busing to ensure racial mixing in all schools regardless of residential segregation.[12] It is beyond the scope of this paper to assess the political, legal, and financial costs of such a scheme, or its implications for the health and education of children.

In establishing a baseline we shall focus on the sorting effects of several bureaucratic processes endemic to conventional public school systems.[13] These include student assignment and resource allocation processes that lead disadvantaged children to experience: racially isolated schools; less money per pupil and less capable teachers; restricted access to instructional programs that enhance life opportunities; enhanced access to instructional programs that limit life opportunities.

---

[12]Gary Orfield, *Schools More Separate: Consequences of a Decade of Resegregation* (Cambridge Mass.: The Civil Rights Project, Harvard University, 2001), p. 10.

[13]Throughout this chapter we focus on differences in opportunity *within* school districts—not the same thing as differences in opportunity caused by parents' choice of school districts in which to reside. (This is called Tiebout choice; see Hoxby.) These choices are based on fundamental American freedoms that will not become either more or less available no matter how districts allocate children to schools. Parents might move to avoid district policies they consider adverse or to flee groups of students whom they do not want their children to associate with. Residential choice enables these moves, but district policy can cause them. Thus, we cannot confidently assign the outcomes of inter-district moves solely to choice or to district policy.

First, we analyze the ways that each of the harms listed above can occur in conventional public school systems, and summarize the available evidence about how often and how severely these harms actually occur. We then go on to identify the ways in which these same harms can occur under choice programs, and we summarize available evidence about the performance of choice programs. Admittedly, our conclusions in the second section are weakly evidenced and tentative, since existing choice programs are small and are often designed to serve the poor and ensure integration. Universal choice programs, in which every family chooses and every school is a school of choice, might work differently from the exemplars available for study today.

THE HARMS OF THE EXISTING SYSTEM

RACIALLY ISOLATED SCHOOLS

Eliminating segregation by race has been a dominant concern of public school systems since the *Brown* decision in 1954. Every large school system has had a desegregation plan, whether court-ordered or voluntary, and the U.S. Department of Education has monitored racial isolation in every school district large and small. No school district has an overt segregation policy, and most have made significant efforts to create racially mixed student bodies. However, most districts remain segregated to some degree, and segregation has recently increased.[14]

How does this happen? In part it happens because of processes that school systems do not control: housing economics, demographic change, and geography. Low-income families, including the majority of Hispanic and African American households, cluster in neighborhoods with low-cost housing. Wealthier families, most of which are white, avoid living in these neighborhoods. Lower-income

---

[14]See Gary Orfield and John T. Yun, *Resegregation in American Schools* (Cambridge, Mass.: The Civil Rights Project, Harvard University, 1999).

minority families also have more children than higher-income white families. This leads to concentrations of minority children in certain neighborhoods.[15] In many cities (Seattle, for example) transportation between white and minority neighborhoods is complicated by bridges and choked freeways, making it very difficult to move children from one neighborhood to another.

Public school systems can exacerbate these problems by maintaining attendance boundaries that divide neighboring minority and white areas. They can also respond to growing minority enrollments by enlarging schools deep in minority areas rather than by developing new schools in areas accessible to people of all races. They can also create admissions processes for attractive magnet schools that give the advantage to aggressive, articulate, and well-connected middle-class parents. Finally, they can limit the supply of schools that students from all neighborhoods want to attend—for example, by maintaining a fixed set of schools rather than expanding or duplicating magnet schools that have long waiting lists. Taken together, these actions can lead to significant segregation by race and ethnicity.

The Baseline Level of Racially Isolated Schooling
Reports from the Harvard Project on Civil Rights provide data on segregation nationwide. One simple measure is the proportion of white students in schools attended by students of different races. In 1999, the school attended by a typical white student was 81.2 percent white, 8.6 percent African American, 6.6 percent Latino, 2.8 percent Asian, and 0.8 percent American Indian. In contrast, the school attended by a typical African American student was 32.6 percent white and 54.5 percent black. Latinos were even more segregated: the typical Latino student attended a school that was only

---

[15]See, e.g., Gary Orfield, *Schools More Separate: Consequences of a Decade of Resegregation* (Cambridge Mass.: The Civil Rights Project, Harvard University, 2001), p. 28. Orfield does not try to estimate the growth in segregation due to differential fertility.

29.9 percent white.[16] Though school segregation has decreased markedly since 1960, separation of white and minority students has increased since 1988. In the South, as Orfield reports, the proportion of black students enrolled in majority white schools declined from 43.5 percent in 1988 to 32.7 percent in 1998.[17]

Much of the recent growth in segregation has been the result of shifts in student population. In the decade 1988–1998 the number of white students in public schools nationwide declined from 34.7 million to 28.9 million, whereas in the same period the number of minority students rose from 8.3 million to 14.8 million.[18] Changes have been most dramatic in the West, where whites went from 63.3 percent of public school enrollment to 51.9 percent in the eleven-year period 1987–1998. Many big cities have also become minority enclaves. In 1998, white students made up less than 20 percent of the public school population in eighteen of the twenty-five largest cities. Schools in Chicago, Detroit, Dallas, New Orleans, Washington, D.C., and Atlanta are no more than 10 percent white.[19] It is clear that in some localities it is impossible to avoid having some overwhelmingly minority schools.

Segregation is pronounced even in states with few minority students. For example, in 1998, the typical black student in a state in which only one in sixteen students was black was likely to attend a school in which more than one in two students was black; nationwide, in 1998, black students, who made up only 18 percent of the school population, had a 37 percent chance of going to schools where blacks made up more than 90 percent of the student body.[20]

Though data on individual school districts can be hard to find, racial isolation is common. In Louisville, for example,

[16]Orfield and Yun, p. 17.
[17]Orfield 2001, p. 33.
[18]Ibid., p. 20.
[19]Ibid., p. 29.
[20]Ibid., pp. 41, 47.

black students make up 27.4 percent of the high school population, but six of twenty high schools have student bodies
less than 20 percent black and six have student bodies more
than 40 percent black.[21] In Charlotte-Mecklenburg, like
Louisville a city in which white students are in the majority
(54 percent), 27 percent of white students and 18 percent of
blacks were in racially isolated schools. Under Charlotte's
court-ordered definition, a white student is in a racially isolated school if its population is more than 69 percent white.
(The corresponding number for black students is 56 percent
black.)[22] In Charlotte, more than 35 percent of public schools
are racially isolated under the local definition. In a much more
racially unbalanced city, the District of Columbia, whites constitute less than 4.3 percent of the school population, but the
average white student attends a school where the combined
black and Latino population is less than 50 percent.[23]

Individual school districts will vary, but these underlying
facts reflect a common pattern. They set a baseline against
which the segregation effects of choice can be measured.
Choice programs might lead to worse segregation than we
now have—to a situation where, for example, blacks nationwide have a greater than 50 percent chance of attending
schools that are more than 90 percent black, or where the
average white student goes to a school in which even less
than 20 percent of students are black. However, as these
data show, the existing system does not live up to its rhetor-
ical commitment to complete racial mixing. Choice programs should surely be compared against the system's real
performance, not its aspirations.

---

[21]Michal Kurlaender and John T. Yun, *Is Diversity a Compelling Educational
Interest? Evidence from Metropolitan Louisville* (Cambridge Mass.: The Civil
Rights Project, Harvard University, 2000), p. 8.

[22]Data reanalyzed by the present authors from Stephen Samuel Smith and
Roslyn Arlyn Mickelson, "All That Glitters Is Not Gold: School Reform in
Chalotte-Mecklenburg," *Educational Evaluation and Policy Analysis* 22, no. 3
(summer 2000): 101–28.

[23]Orfield 2001, p. 27.

DOLLAR AND HUMAN RESOURCE INEQUITIES

Public school districts receive funds from many sources—local property taxes, their state's basic school funding formula, various state programs that provide money for defined purposes and various federal funding sources—and the districts use these funds in similarly complex ways. Laypersons might expect money to be allocated to schools on a per-pupil basis, but that is not the case. Districts buy things like teachers, books, equipment, expert advice, buses, school construction, and maintenance, and those things are allocated to schools through political and bureaucratic processes. As a result, some schools may receive much higher funding allocations, and much more valuable resources, than others.

The most valuable resource allocated in this way is the teaching staff. In virtually all school districts, teachers allocate themselves to schools, and the most senior and highest-paid teachers get first choice. The majority of senior teachers choose schools in the "nicer" neighborhoods. The result is that the teachers who work in schools with the most advantaged students are, on average, much more highly paid than teachers who work in the poorer ends of town. Nor are the poorer students compensated for this difference in average teacher salaries; rather, the district's public accounts average out the salaries of all teachers so it is not evident that the schools with many expensive senior teachers have any more money than the schools with many cheap new teachers. On a real-dollar basis, per-pupil expenditures are much higher in the schools chosen by senior teachers.

Though staff salaries constitute as much as 80 percent of school-level expenditure, districts allocate other resources to schools. Poor schools get disproportionate shares of the 10 percent of funds that come from federal and state programs intended for low-income students. This does only a little to compensate for the expenditure differences associated with teacher allocation.

Funds for the education of children with disabilities are allocated on the basis of diagnoses of children's needs, and in this parent initiative is a major factor, since more sophisticated parents are more likely than the less aware to demand and get expensive individualized placements for their children with disabilities. Low-income and minority children identified with disabilities are therefore much more likely to be assigned to self-contained special education classrooms for mental retardation or emotional disturbance than to be "mainstreamed" in general education classrooms and receive related services.[24] Districts also control resources such as computers and science lab equipment maintenance funds, and these are allocated on a "squeaky wheel" basis. Schools having respected principals and teachers, as well as active and well-connected parents, can capture disproportionate shares of these resources. Though district accounting makes it extremely difficult to compute real-dollar per pupil expenditures, within-district resource allocation consistently favors the more aggressive and influential families and neighborhoods.

The Baseline Level of Resource Inequity

The existing system allocates the two most important resources in education—dollars and quality teachers—by bureaucratic means. The result is dramatic inequity within school districts.[25] Analyzing school funding in Seattle, Marguerite Roza found that elementary schools in poverty

---

[24]T. Parrish (draft proposal). *Disparities in the Identification, Funding, and Provision of Special Education,* submitted to the Civil Rights Project for the Conference on Minority Issues in Special Education in Public Schools. <http://csef.air.org/civrights.html>.

[25]Since the early 1970s there has been a research and litigation industry focused on differences in per-pupil expenditure among the school districts in a state. Courts have repeatedly found that state policies leading to unequal per-pupil funding violate the equal protection clause of the Fourteenth Amendment to the U.S. Constitution. This industry has largely ignored the dramatic differences in spending and resource allocation *within* school districts. Presumably, the same constitutional principles could be applied to the inequities identified in this section.

neighborhoods often received real-dollar resources worth as much as $300,000 less than was claimed by the district's budget, and that similarly sized schools in high-income neighborhoods got correspondingly more money than the district budget acknowledged. This was the result of a combination of placement privileges for senior teachers—which allow senior teachers to cluster in schools in higher-income neighborhoods—and average teacher costing, which charges schools the same amount for every teacher whatever the teacher's actual salary. Under such a scheme, schools in nice neighborhoods get a more expensive teaching force than they could afford if they paid real prices for teachers, and schools in poorer neighborhoods get a much cheaper teaching force.[26]

When Houston school officials computed real-dollar spending in their high schools they were shocked to learn that one school in a predominantly white section of town had one million dollars more to spend each year than a school of the same size in a minority area. The difference, they learned, was entirely due to differences in teacher pay, because teachers in the higher-spending white school, who were older and more experienced, ranked higher on the pay scale.[27]

It is important to note that Seattle and Houston are not isolated incidents when it comes to inequalities in school funding. State-by-state data from the Education Trust indicate that schools with a high percentage of low-income students receive anywhere from $32 to $2,700 less per student than schools with a low percentage of low-income students; a disparity in funding was found in 42 out of the 49 states studied.[28]

Lack of access to qualified teachers also produces inequalities between racial and socioeconomic groups. In California,

---

[26]Marguerite Roza, "Creating Local Data Analysis Capacity", in Paul T. Hill, ed., *New Institutions for Education Reform* (Washington D.C.: Brookings Institution Press: forthcoming, 2002).

[27]Personal communication with Dr. Susan Sclafani, former Houston Deputy Superintendent of Schools.

[28]Education Watch Online: New State and National Achievement Gap Report. The Education Trust. <www.edtrust.org>.

the number of economically disadvantaged students in a school is positively correlated with the number of teachers having the least amount of teaching experience and holding a bachelor's degree or less.[29] This correlation is particularly strong in the elementary grades. In secondary education, national data indicate that 25 percent of classes in high-poverty schools are taught by teachers who lack a major or minor in the field they teach, compared with 15 percent of classes in low-poverty schools.[30] This disparity is even greater for math, where only 25 percent of the teachers in high-poverty schools were majors in math, compared with 40 percent of higher-income schools.[31]

Inequalities also exist based on racial composition. In schools where the student population is over 90 percent white, 69 percent of teachers have BAs or higher in math versus 42 percent in schools where 90 percent or more of students are part of a minority group.[32] National data show similar disparities, with 22 percent of teachers in high-minority secondary schools lacking a major or minor in the field they teach, compared with 16 percent of teachers in low-minority schools.[33]

When examining the differences in human resources among schools, it is important to address the negative results of ineffective teachers. These results can be found at both the elementary and secondary levels. In Dallas, fifth-grade students who had three consecutive ineffective teachers showed gains of only 29 percent in math scores, compared with an 83 percent gain for students with three years of effective teachers. In Boston, high school students had average gains of −0.6

[29]J. R. Betts, K. S. Rueben, and A. Danenberg. "Equal Resources, Equal Outcomes? The Distribution of School Resources and Student Achievement in California" (Public Policy Institute of California, 2000).

[30]Education Watch Online Web site.

[31]Kati Haycock et al., *Achievement in America 2000* (Washington D.C.: The Education Trust, 2000).

[32]J. Oakes, *Multiplying Inequalities: The Effects of Race, Social Class, and Tracking on Opportunities to Learn Mathematics and Science* (Santa Monica, Calif.: Rand Corporation, 1990).

[33]Education Watch Online.

in math and 0.3 in reading after one year with ineffective teachers, compared with students with effective teachers, who had average gains of 14.6 and 5.6, respectively.[34]

ALLOCATION OF OPPORTUNITY-LIMITING PROGRAMS

The fact that students come to school with different amounts of prior knowledge and different abilities presents problems for teachers, schools, and districts. The preceding section on segregation focused on how students are allocated among schools. This section focuses on how students are allocated to classes and programs within schools. Teachers find it difficult to prepare lessons and oversee learning for students with very diverse prior experiences and ability. Parents of the more advanced students worry that teaching will be tailored to the needs of others, and that their children will consequently learn less than they might. Parents of the less-advanced students are also forthright in demanding that their children get extra help and attention. The response by public schools and school districts is to differentiate instruction and create homogeneous classroom groups. The federal and state governments also provide special funding for instruction for defined groups, especially low-achieving students, children in poverty, and the handicapped.

Some differentiation of instruction is inevitable; some might even be desirable. But there are ways in which differentiation can harm minority and disadvantaged students. Removing students from regular classrooms to get special drills and tutoring can mean that they never master the material that others are learning while they are away.[35] Reducing contact with advanced students can eliminate a potential learning opportunity, and creating programs that

---

[34]Ibid.

[35]J. Kimbrough and P. T. Hill. *The Aggregate Effects of Federal Education Programs* (Santa Monica, Calif.: Rand Corporation, 1981). Also see Anthony S. Bryk, Valerie Lee, and Patrick Holland, *Catholic Schools and the Common Good* (Cambridge, Mass.: Harvard University Press, 1993); and P. T. Hill, G. Foster, and T. Gendler, *High Schools with Character* (Santa Monica, Calif.: Rand Corporation, 1990).

focus on low-level skills can discourage children who, though at some disadvantage, are excited about ideas and could be motivated by highly challenging instruction. Moreover, low-status programs may discourage both teachers as well as students and set off a downward spiral of expectations and performance.

There has been a long debate about the educational value and ethical acceptability of the combination of ability grouping and program differentiation,[36] but there is little dispute about the fact that some students are assigned to such programs on the basis of color and family background, and that there can be significant overlaps in the ability of students assigned to less and more challenging programs. Nor is there any doubt that students assigned to some such programs are extremely unlikely to finish their K–12 education. The current system, by the way it designs special instructional programs and assigns students to them, puts some students at a grave disadvantage.

The Baseline Allocation of
Opportunity-Limiting Programs

U.C.L.A. education researcher Jeannie Oakes is the most important source of data on the assignment of students to opportunity-limiting courses, called tracking. In her 1985 book *Keeping Track* she shows that schools with different instructional programs for students considered faster and slower consistently assign minority and low-income students to the slower tracks.[37] Though track placement is meant to correlate with student performance on achievement tests and grades in previous classes, Oakes reports significant overlap in ability among children in different tracks. She cites a high school in Rockford, Illinois, in which the math scores of students in high-track courses ranged from the 26th to the 99th

---

[36]See T. Loveless, *The Tracking Wars: State Reform Meets School Policy* (Washington, D.C.: Brookings Institution Press, 1990).

[37]J. Oakes, *Keeping Track: How Schools Structure Inequality* (New Haven, Conn.: Yale University Press, 1985).

percentile on national achievement tests; in the same school, the scores of students assigned to lower tracks ranged between the 1st and 99th percentile.[38] Oakes reports similar score patterns in various subjects throughout most of the middle and high schools in the Rockford and San Jose, California, districts.

In many cases, race and class appear to be better predictors of track placement than any academic measure. For example, Oakes found that in San Jose, white students with average scores in national math tests were three times more likely to be placed in high-track math courses than were Latino students with similar scores. The discrepancies for students with higher scores are even more striking: for students scoring between 90th and 99th percentile on national tests, only 56 percent of Latinos were placed in high-track courses, compared with 93 percent of whites and 97 percent of Asians. Similar patterns of discrimination were found at the senior and junior high levels in Rockford.[39]

In a district in Southern California, 88 percent of white students who scored in the top quartile on the Comprehensive Test of Basic Skills were placed in algebra classes; but only 42 percent of Latino and 51 percent of African American students who scored in the top quartile were placed in algebra. For students who scored in the second quartile, 11 percent of Latino and 16 percent of African American students were placed in algebra, compared with 83 percent of Asian and 53 percent of white students.[40] Roslyn Mickelson found similar patterns in the Charlotte-Mecklenburg school district, where white students were far more likely than black students of equal tested ability to be assigned to higher mathematics, laboratory science, and advanced courses in English and history.

---

[38]J. Oakes, "Two Cities' Tracking and Within-School Segregation," *Teachers College Record* 96, no. 4 (1995): 681–90.

[39]Ibid.

[40]Unpublished paper by the Achievement Council, Inc., Los Angeles, 1991, cited in *Achievement in America, 2000*, The Education Trust, Inc. <http://204.176.179.36/dc/edtrust/edstart.cfm>.

These results held even when the researchers controlled for students' prior achievement, level of effort, and parents' education.[41] In another study, Oakes found that the same student might be in one track or another depending on the district or school he or she attends. Students who might be allocated to a college preparatory track in one school district were likely to be assigned to dead-end general or vocational tracks in another.[42]

Placement in lower tracks virtually guarantees that students are taught more slowly, are exposed to more rudimentary content, and receive high grades for work that would in other settings be considered unacceptable. For example, Oakes found that students in low-track science and mathematics courses were given more worksheets, tests, and other rote forms of instruction than the average- and high-track students. She also reports that students in high-track classes at a disadvantaged school frequently have less qualified teachers than students in low-track courses at a more advantaged school.[43] Mickelson found that students in lower tracks are more likely to have teachers who lack training in the field they are teaching.[44] Several authors have documented the consequences of track placement for students' academic success, high school graduation, completion of higher education, and lifelong income chances. Recently, Heather Rose and Julian Betts have shown how valuable exposure to rigorous college preparatory courses, especially advanced mathematics, can be for minority students.[45]

Besides tracking, labeling students with disabilities is another way schools can separate students from higher-level courses. A

---

[41]R. A. Mickelson, "Subverting Swann: First- and Second-Generation Segregation in the Charlotte-Mecklenburg Schools," *American Education Research Journal* 38, no. 2 (2001): 215–52.

[42]J. Oakes and G. Guiton, "Matchmaking: The Dynamics of High School Tracking Decision," *American Educational Research Journal* 32, no. 1 (1995): 3–33.

[43]J. Oakes, *Multiplying Inequalities: The Effects of Race, Social Class, and Tracking on Opportunities to Learn Mathematics and Science* (Santa Monica, Calif.: Rand Corporation, 1990).

[44]Mickelson 2001, p. 238.

[45]Rose and Betts, *Math Matters*.

state-by-state analysis by T. Parrish found that in thirty-eight states, African American students were more than twice as likely as white students to be identified as mentally retarded.[46] In twenty-nine states, African American students were more than twice as likely to be identified as emotionally disturbed. Nationally, although African American students account for 14.8 percent of the school-age population, they account for 34.3 percent of students identified with mental retardation and 26.4 percent of students identified as emotionally disturbed.[47] Students labeled in these ways are usually separated from regular classes and taught in "resource rooms" in which instruction focuses on low-level skills. The likelihood of being labeled mentally retarded or emotionally disturbed does seem to vary from district to district. D. P. Oswald and colleagues found that districts with the lowest proportions of African American students are the most likely to identify those students as emotionally disturbed.[48] According to Ladner and Hammons, in predominantly white districts in Texas, nearly one in four African American students is assigned to special education.[49]

Even more than placement in lower academic tracks, assignment to special education marks students for academic

---

[46]T. Parrish, "Disparities in the Identification, Funding, and Provision of Special Education," submitted to the Civil Rights Project for the Conference on Minority Issues in Special Education in Public Schools. <http://csef.air.org/civrights.html>.

[47]U. S. Department of Education, Office of Special Education Programs, Twenty-second Annual Report to Congress on the Individuals with Disabilities Education Act (2000); <http://www.ed.gov/offices/OSERS/OSEP/OSEP2000AnlRpt/>.

[48]D. P. Oswald, M. J. Coutinho, A. M. Best, and N. N. Singh, "Ethnic Representation in Special Education: The Influence of School-Related Economic and Demographic Variables," *Journal of Special Education* 32, no. 4 (1999): 194–206.

[49]In studies of district data from Texas and Florida, Ladner and Hammons also found that race influences special education rates more than other predictor variables such as poverty, student-teacher ratio, spending per pupil, and teacher salaries. The effect of race is almost double the next highest variable (poverty) and is stronger than the combination of the other three variables in this study. They also present data suggesting that African American and Hispanic students' placement rate in special education is nearly 10 percent higher in predominately white districts than in predominately minority districts. M. Ladner and C. Hammons, "Special But Unequal: Race and Special Education," in Finn, Rotherham, and Hokanson, eds., *Rethinking Special Education for a New Century* (Fordham Foundation and the Progressive Policy Institute, 2001).

failure. According to the National Longitudinal Transition Study of Special Education, African Americans identified as emotionally and behaviorally disturbed had a 66 percent failure rate in school; the failure rate for whites so labeled was 38 percent. African American students with EBD were twice as likely to exit school by dropping out (58.2 percent) as by graduating (27.5 percent).[50]

We do not claim that lower track placements and assignment to special education are always inappropriate; certainly some students do better in those programs than they would in regular or advanced classrooms. However, as these data show, conventional public education uses low-track placement and disability labels liberally, especially for disadvantaged students. The result is often a kind of segregation more complete, and more consequential, for minority students than segregation based openly on race.

MISALLOCATION OF OPPORTUNITY-EXPANDING PROGRAMS

An awareness of the obligation to teach all students to read and do basic arithmetic defines most elementary schools, and limits the degree to which they can differ from one another. Among the public elementary schools in a given district, the most important differences are due to variations in staff quality, or to school culture difference resulting from habits of staff interaction. Beyond those differences, some schools get programs that others do not. Not every school gets a special program for gifted and talented students. Many districts offer one or two schools designed on a distinctive model of instruction, like Montessori. Gifted programs and special schools based on brand-name instructional approaches are allocated on a squeaky-wheel basis, to neighborhoods with

---

[50]L. A. Valdes, C. L. Williamson, and M. M. Wagner, "The National Longitudinal Study of Special Education Students, *Statistical Almanac*, vol. 3: *Youth Categorized as Emotionally Disturbed* (Menlo Park, Calif.: SRI International, 1990), as cited in D. Osher, D. Woodruff, and A. Sims, "Exploring Relationships Between Inappropriate and Ineffective Special Education Services for African American Children and Youth and the Overrepresentation in the Juvenile Justice System," draft paper available at <www.law.harvard.edu/civilrights/conferences/SpecEd/osherpaper2.html>.

activist parents or to areas of town where parents are beginning to depart for private or suburban schools. Thus in most districts, such programs and districts are disproportionately available to middle-class, usually white, children.

High schools have much more varied programs. Not every school has excellent laboratories, an array of advanced placement courses, or enough qualified teachers of mathematics, science, or languages to allow every student to pursue an advanced college preparatory course. In many schools these opportunities are allocated in part by traditional patterns in course enrollment—an approach that may sound reasonable but can create a watering-down of instructional opportunities, so that students in a school where few students have over the years taken advanced courses lose their opportunity to explore such courses. These opportunities are also allocated in response to family and neighborhood pressure, which further favors schools serving middle-class students.

This process is not always one way, however. Urban districts facing criticism about low-performing schools in poor neighborhoods sometimes transfer reputedly "successful" principals from middle-class neighborhoods to these schools. Families in the "nicer" schools often feel deprived in this way, and schools often face difficult adjustments when a principal is pulled out of a smoothly functioning school.

The Baseline Allocation of
Opportunity-Expanding Programs

Nationally, both African American and Hispanic children are much less likely to be assigned to gifted programs than students from other groups. According to the Office of Civil Rights (OCR), in 1992 African American students were 57 percent as likely, and Hispanic students 58 percent as likely, as children from other groups to be considered gifted.[51] Economically disadvantaged students are also significantly underrepresented in

---

[51]D. Y. Ford, "The Underrepresentation of Minority Students in Gifted Education: Problems and Promises in Recruitment and Retention," *Journal of Special Education* 32, no. 1 (1998): 4–14.

gifted education. Only 9 percent of students in gifted and talented education programs were in the bottom quartile of family income, while 47 percent of program participants were
from the top quartile in family income.[52]

Another measure of minority students' separation from opportunity-expanding programs is their low participation in advanced placement (AP) courses. These are often the most
advanced courses offered by high schools, and students who attain high scores on national tests can gain college credit. Nationally, African American and Latino students are far less likely
than white and Asian students to take AP courses. Statewide AP
data for Texas also fit this pattern. In 1998–99, 10.9 percent of
all high school students, but only 4.2 percent of African American and 7.1 percent of Hispanic students, took AP courses.
However, African Americans and Hispanics are also less likely
than others to score 3 or above on the tests: 31 percent and 48
percent compared with 58 percent of all AP-takers.[53]

To some degree, these figures may reflect differences among
school districts, especially since minority students cluster in
districts that offer only a few—if any—AP courses. Within-
district data are more telling about the consequences of bureaucratic processes. Bernhole and colleagues have shown that
for one district (Wake County, North Carolina) African
American students make up 24 percent of the high school
population but only 3.5 percent of students taking AP examinations.[54] The corresponding percentages for Hispanic students are 2.3 and 1.8, and for whites, 70 and 78. Of course,
AP courses are meant only for well-prepared students, so that
enrollment differences might reflect the numbers of different
groups prepared for these courses. This might explain some of

---

[52]National Education Longitudinal Study (NELS) of 1988 in National Center
for Education Statistics, *Urban Schools: The Challenge of Locational Poverty*
(Washington, D.C.: U.S. Department of Education, 1996).
[53]Texas Education Agency, Office of Policy Planning and Research. *Advanced
Placement and International Baccalaureate Examination Results in Texas,
1998–99* (2000).
[54]A. Bernholc, N. Baenen, and R. Howell, *Measuring Up: 1998-99 Advanced
Placement Exam Results* (Wake County Public Schools, Evaluation and Research
Department, 2000).

the exclusion of black students, since only 56 percent of those who took AP courses (compared with 78 percent of white students) got scores equal to or above 3, usually considered the threshold for college credit. This pattern is reversed, however, for Hispanic students: 87 percent of those who took AP courses made scores of 3 or above.

Oakes and colleagues had similar findings when comparing low- and high-income neighborhood schools in the Los Angeles Unified School District. Of twelve very large high schools in low-income neighborhoods, only 639 students took AP exams in math and science and only 18 percent, or 117 students, earned a score of 3 or above. Conversely, five high schools in the district's high-income neighborhoods had 890 students take the math and science AP exams, with 71 percent, or 629 students, receiving a pass score.

Table 1 summarizes what we have learned about the baseline against which choice programs should be compared.

TABLE 1
Our Best Estimates on Incidence of Segregated
Placements and Resource Inequities

Category of Comparison	Current System Performance
Racially isolated schools	Schools often exceed district-wide average proportion black or white by 20% or more
Inequitable allocation of dollars and teachers	Most experienced and expensive teachers cluster in "nicest" neighborhoods; per pupil expenditures unequal
Inequitable allocation of opportunity-expanding programs	White and middle-class children 3 times more likely to enroll in gifted and AP programs
Inequitable allocation of opportunity-limiting programs	Minority and lower-income children 3 times more likely to be enrolled in lower tracks and out-of-class special education

The next section summarizes what little we know about the effects of choice programs.

WHAT IS KNOWN ABOUT CHOICE PROGRAMS

Choice programs, whether based on vouchers or on school chartering, must confront the same realities that limit the current system: economics, neighborhood segregation, fertility trends, and costs of transportation. Critics and supporters of choice differ on whether it is likely to increase or decrease segregation and inequities in the allocation of dollars, quality teachers, and opportunity-limiting or opportunity-expanding programs.

With Respect to Segregation. Critics of choice fear that it can exacerbate the problem by allowing privileged families to take advantage of their superior access to information to select the best schools; by tolerating admissions processes that let privileged families monopolize access to the most attractive schools; and by allowing the most sought-after schools to handpick the easiest-to-educate students.

Defenders of choice programs would respond that these abuses could be eliminated by good program design. Choice programs can promote desegregation in ways conventional public school systems do not—by encouraging out-of-neighborhood school placement, by allowing the formation of new schools accessible to students in overcrowded schools, and by encouraging expansion or reproduction of oversubscribed schools.

With Respect to Dollar and Human Resource Inequities. Critics fear that choice will lead to heavier financing of schools preferred by privileged families, and concentration of the ablest teachers in schools with the most money and the most rewarding students.

Defenders of choice point out that voucher and charter plans all start with transparent allocation of dollars to schools and equality of per pupil spending. Supply-side choice also constrains schools to live within defined real-dollar budgets, so that no school can afford to hire all the highest-paid teachers. Choice supporters admit, however, that there is nothing to prevent schools with the best reputations from hiring the very best teachers or using their funds much more efficiently than other schools.

With Respect to Opportunity-Limiting Programs. Schools of choice could come under the same pressures as existing public schools, to avoid slowing down faster students by creating lower-track programs for the disadvantaged. Organizations that ran networks of several schools (for example, charter school networks or Catholic archdioceses) could also create specialty schools targeted to children of different ability levels. Some "special" schools and programs might become unchallenging and low status, and students might be assigned to them on the basis of race or social class.

Defenders of choice argue that competition makes these results unlikely: schools that create highly differentiated programs will be inefficient and lose out to schools that offer a limited number of focused courses;[55] and families will leave schools that put their children in dead-end courses. There is some favorable evidence about existing schools of choice: charter schools and parochial schools offer more restricted sets of courses than public schools, and parochial schools make sure that disadvantaged students experience mainstream college prep courses.[56] These facts, however, apply to a limited number of schools of choice, most of them operated by groups with strong commitments to social justice. No one can say for sure whether some schools in a much larger school choice sector might allocate minority students to opportunity-limiting programs.

With Respect to Opportunity-Expanding Programs. Under any choice scheme, entrepreneurs (charter school

---

[55]See Hill, "The Supply Side of Choice."

[56]See James S. Coleman and Thomas Hoffer, *Public and Private High Schools* (New York: Basic Books, 1987). See also James Coleman, Thomas Hoffer, and Sally Kilgore, *High School Achievement: Public, Catholic, and Private Schools Compared* (New York: Basic Books, 1982).

operators, nonprofit organizations, for-profit contractors) could choose to locate their schools in areas more accessible to "easy to educate" children. Competition will naturally limit the number of schools that can succeed by this strategy, but poorer neighborhoods could still get more "bare bones" schools. This could happen for two reasons: school providers could decide that there is insufficient demand for advanced courses of study in poorer neighborhoods; and organizations running more than one school could try to run lower-cost operations in poorer neighborhoods in order to subsidize the more excellent programs needed to compete in richer neighborhoods.

Defenders of choice argue that school providers have a strong incentive to demonstrate that they can serve the populations that public schools now serve badly. They point to evidence, such as that provided by John Chubb in Chapter 4 of this book, that organizations that manage many schools of choice serve a lower-income and more heavily minority clientele than their surrounding school districts.[57]

WHY EVIDENCE ON THE EFFECTS OF CHOICE IS LIMITED

Empirical evidence is thin on all sides of these arguments. Current voucher and charter school programs are small in scale and many are focused on serving poor and minority children. The results of those programs show that some independently run schools will serve the disadvantaged. But they do not prove that systems of universal choice would have the same benign results.

---

[57]With respect to charter schools, see U.S. Department of Education, *The State of Charter Schools 2000* (Washington, D.C.: January 2000), esp. sec. C, p. 2. Nationally, white students make up 48 percent of the charter school population compared with 58 percent of the population served by conventional public schools. Charter school student populations are disproportionately white in Arizona, California, Colorado, and Georgia, and disproportionately minority in Florida, Massachusetts, Michigan, Minnesota, New Jersey, North Carolina, Pennsylvania, Texas, and Wisconsin.

The evidence is also incomplete in another way: current voucher and charter programs do not have the kinds of supply-side effects that universal choice programs are likely to have. Groups that start new schools must now accept less money per pupil than public schools get, and they know that the charter or voucher program on which they rely could be canceled almost at any time. Starting a new school would be a much easier proposition if children came with the full public per pupil expenditure and if choice programs were stable. Until such a program exists we cannot know how many new schools will arise, or what courses of instruction they will offer, or whom they will serve.[58]

It is important to say why the evidence is so thin. Most choice-oriented policies, including charter school laws and voucher initiatives, are constructed politically. Groups like teachers unions and school administrators associations oppose such policies, but when it is obvious that some forms of choice will be permitted, they focus on limiting their size and scope.[59] An example of this was the success of groups opposing the original voucher program in Alum Rock, California, who were able to constrain it so that few parents had choices and few new schooling options were created.[60] Today, groups opposing voucher programs work to limit the numbers of families that may choose and the numbers of schools that can be chosen. Opponents also work to limit the amount of money that follows children to schools of choice, often ensuring that charter schools and private schools accepting vouchers receive less money per pupil than is spent in local public school districts. Moreover, teachers unions

---

[58]The British experience with choice shows that large-scale choice programs have much more equitable effects than do small-scale programs, and that results become more equitable the longer a choice program is in place. See Gorard, Fitz, and Taylor, "School Choice Impacts."

[59]See R. C. Bulman and D. L. Kirp, "The Shifting Politics of School Choice," in Sugarman and Kremerer, eds., *Choice and School Controversy.*

[60]See Stephen S. Weiner and Konrad Kellan, *The Politics and Administration of the Voucher Demonstration in Alum Rock, The First Year, 1972–1973* (Santa Monica, Calif.: Rand Corporation, 1974).

and school boards often unite to cushion public schools
from the financial impact of losing students.[61] Taken together, such constraints limit what can be learned from
choice programs. Limits on who may choose schools can
bias choice programs—in some cases toward serving disproportionate numbers of poor or minority children, and in
some cases toward excluding poor families that cannot pay
extra tuition or provide volunteer services that underfunded
schools must require.

Table 2 illustrates the kinds of constraints that have been
imposed on choice programs, on both the supply and demand sides. No wonder the evidence about how choice
would work in the real world is so limited.

CONCLUSION

Until a serious choice experiment is tried—one that is large
and long-lasting enough to gauge supply-side effects as well as
families' decisions—we cannot be certain whether choice
would provide worse outcomes than the current system, nor
can we say how tightly choice must be regulated. For the time
being, however, it appears that those who oppose choice and
defend the current public system have failed to recognize that
they, not the proponents of choice, must bear the burden of
proof. Opponents condemn choice because it creates opportunities for alert and aggressive parents to gain the best of
everything for their children. They argue that choice is risky
and that the existing public education system is a safer and
more just alternative. However, as this chapter has shown, the
existing public education system, which restricts choice by assigning children to schools and limiting the supply of available
publicly funded schools, does not accomplish desegregation or
give disadvantaged children equitable access to good schools.
Public school systems are segregated, particularly in the big

---

[61]See National Governors' Association, *Strategic Investment: Tough Choices for America's Future* (Washington, D.C., 1993).

TABLE 2

Constraints That Reduce the Evidence Value of Choice Programs

Supply-side Constraints	Demand-side Constraints
Rules limiting the numbers of schools of choice that may be created [a, f]	Limits on the numbers of students (or the percentage of students in a locality) who may choose schools [a, b, c, f]
Rules preventing private groups from operating publicly funded schools [a, d]	Rules eliminating former private school students from receiving vouchers [b]
School board refusal to approve more than token numbers of charters [e]	Rules allowing only students with certain characteristics (e.g., poverty or racial minority status) to choose schools [b, c]
Laws allowing only existing public schools to receive charters [d]	Limits on the neighborhoods from which a family may choose schools [a, d]
Regulations controlling who may teach in schools, what methods they employ, and how they use time and money [a, d]	"Legacy" arrangements that give families who live near a school first choice of whether to attend it [a]
Lower per pupil funding for vouchers or for charter schools (relative to district-run schools [b, c, f]	Rules limiting family choice only to schools that will accept small vouchers (less than public per pupil expenditure) as full tuition [b, c]

Legend:

[a]Alum Rock voucher program; see, for example, J. R. Henig, *Rethinking School Choice: Limits of the Market Metaphor* (Princeton, N.J.: Princeton University Press, 1994).

[b]State-funded voucher programs in Milwaukee and Cleveland; see P. E. Peterson, J. Greene, and C. Noyes, "School Choice in Milwaukee." *Public Interest* 125 (1996): 38-56.

[c]Private voucher programs, e.g., those sponsored by CEO America.

[d]Weak charter school laws, e.g., Georgia's; see P. T. Hill and R. J. Lake, *Charter Schools and Accountability in Public Education* (Washington D.C.: Brookings Institution Press, 2002), ch. 4. See also B. Hassel, *The Charter School Challenge: Avoiding the Pitfalls, Fulfilling the Promise* (Washington, D.C.: Brookings Institution Press, 1999), and Center for Education Reform, *Charter School Laws Across the States* (2001), <http://edreform.com/charter_schools/laws/>

[e]Charter school laws that do not establish criteria for school board approval of charters.

[f]Virtually all charter school laws.

cities where poor and minority children are most concentrated. This is so in spite of decades of serious effort and unwavering declaratory policy in favor of desegregation and equity.

The existing public education system also creates inequities that are unlikely to occur under choice: it allows the best-paid teachers to cluster in middle-class schools, causing serious within-district inequities in per pupil spending. It allocates excellent learning opportunities, including advanced placement courses and programs for the gifted, disproportionately to schools serving higher-income children of well-educated parents. It assigns poor and minority students disproportionately to low-track courses, and assigns minority children, particularly African American males, to forms of special education that separate them from regular classes and virtually guarantee that they will drop out before graduating from high school.

Not all these actions on the part of the existing public education system are unambiguously harmful: some children benefit from placement outside the college prep sequence and some children need treatment for emotional disturbance even if that means they miss class. Any system of publicly funded education, whether based on universal choice or run by a public monopoly, would need some special programs for severely disruptive children or children who need unusual forms of instruction. However, given the radical forms of "sorting" prevalent in existing public school systems, it is hard to see how choice could produce worse segregation, resource inequity, denial of access to excellent programs, or assignment to opportunity-limiting programs than the current system.

Choice programs must not be ruled out because they can lead to some inequities. Every system of allocating opportunities known to man creates some inequities. No matter how opportunities are allocated, parents will seek the best for their own children. Systems should be designed to minimize inequities, and programs should be compared according to the scope and seriousness of inequities they permit. In particular, choice programs must be carefully designed to prevent segregation, and any program that produces levels of segregation as great as those now prevailing in the public education system should be scrapped or redesigned.[62] As later chapters in this book will show, there are ways to regulate both the demand and the supply sides of choice to prevent discrimination more effectively than do the bureaucratic processes of conventional public school systems.

---

[62]Among serious analysts even those most worried about choice admit that ensuring equity is a matter of thoughtful program design. From Casey D. Cobb and Gene V. Glass, "Ethnic Segregation in Arizona Charter Schools," *Education Policy Analysis Archives* 7, no. 1 (January 14, 1999): "The social consequences of choice in education are mediated by the policies under which choice operates. Depending on the degree of public oversight, choice can serve contradictory purposes. Consider two extreme scenarios. Under regulated conditions, choice can correct for severe levels of segregation and ensure the stable integration of schools (e.g., controlled open enrollment plans, magnet programs). Minneapolis, Minnesota, and Cambridge, Massachusetts, endorse such policies. Conversely, unregulated choice can intensify ethnic stratification by allowing parents to remove their children from integrated schools (e.g., white flight). Arizona's laissez-faire charter legislation appears to fall in this latter group."

3

Who Chooses? Who Uses?
Participation in a National School Voucher Program

*Paul E. Peterson, David E. Campbell, and
Martin R. West*

Among the most controversial issues in the heated public
debate over school vouchers is the question of which families
are most likely to leave the public sector and enroll their children in private schools if given the opportunity. Critics assert
that the parents most likely to opt for vouchers will be those
who are already most involved in their children's education—
which, on average, will mean the parents of the most motivated
and gifted students. They also argue that the introduction
of a voucher system would increase the separation of students
by race and social class, with minority and low-income students relegated to underfunded and increasingly neglected
public schools. Proponents, on the other hand, contend that
any "creaming" from the public school system that would
occur as a result of most potential voucher systems would be

The authors wish to thank the operators of the Children's Scholarship
Fund for their cooperation in this evaluation. Caroline Minter Hoxby and
Jay Greene served as consultants to the evaluation. Funding for this study
has been provided by the BASIC Fund Foundation, the Lynde and Harry
Bradley Foundation, the Milton and Rose D. Friedman Foundation, the
Gordon and Laura Gund Foundation, and the John M. Olin Foundation.
The findings and interpretations reported herein are the sole responsibility
of the authors and are not subject to the approval of the program operators
or sources of financial support.

relatively modest. Moreover, they suggest that vouchers would actually serve to reduce racial and socioeconomic segregation by diminishing the salience of parental income and residential location in determining which school a child attends.

INTRODUCTION

This chapter takes advantage of the recent establishment of the Children's Scholarship Fund (CSF), a privately funded national school voucher program targeted at low-income families, to address these issues with quality data. Specifically, we offer answers to two related questions: (1) which eligible families initially chose to apply for a scholarship to attend a private school (*who chooses?*), and (2) among those families who were offered a CSF scholarship, who actually used it to attend a private school (*who uses*)? Together, the answers to these questions allow us to anticipate the short-term impact of the establishment of at least one possible voucher system on the relative compositions of the public and private sectors.

All school voucher proposals involve the distribution of government grants designed to help parents purchase education for their children in schools outside the public sector. However, the range of possible voucher alternatives is substantial. Because the specific design of a voucher system can affect its impact on students and society, any conclusions about the impacts of a particular program must be limited to those that share its essential characteristics.

In this regard, the privately funded CSF program is of interest, because its design is not essentially different from many that have been proposed and implemented as public policy. Most important, the program focuses exclusively on families with low-to-moderate incomes, with the value of the tuition discount offered to families scaled to reflect their relative financial need. In order to be eligible to receive a CSF scholarship, applicants needed to have at least one child in grades K–8 and a total household income of less than 270 percent of the federally determined poverty line for a family of their size. The value of the scholarships applicants received was a function of their income level, household size, and the cost of tuition at the private school they selected: families with an annual household income below the federally established poverty line for a family of their size qualified for scholarships covering up to 75 percent of tuition at the private school of their choice. Families with incomes above this threshold were only eligible to receive awards equal to 50 percent of their tuition payments, and the maximum award for those families with incomes greater than 185 percent of the poverty line fell to just 25 percent of tuition. If a family won the lottery, each of their children in the appropriate grade range was offered a scholarship.

Families awarded CSF scholarships were able to use them to send their children to religious schools; in fact, over 92 percent of parents participating in the program reported that their child attended a private school with a religious affiliation.[1] Because the value of the scholarship was never allowed to exceed 75 percent of the full cost of tuition, and was often much less, parents were effectively forced to use their own funds to supplement their award. No upper limit was placed on the amount of money they could use for this purpose.

Many of these characteristics of the CSF correspond quite closely to those of local programs in Cleveland and Milwaukee, the two largest and longest-running government-funded voucher systems currently in existence in the United States. A proposal to create a similar program on a national scale was debated in the House of Representatives as recently as 1997.[2] Finally, Terry Moe's recent study of national public opinion regarding school vouchers suggests that Americans

[1]P. E. Peterson and D. E. Campbell, "An Evaluation of the Children's Scholarship Fund." Working paper, Program on Education Policy and Governance, Harvard University, 2001.

[2]Helping Empower Low-Income Parents (HELP) Scholarship Amendments, H.R. 2746, 1997.

would be most likely to support a voucher program if it initially has each of the features outlined above.[3] If a voucher system is to prove politically feasible, therefore, whether on a national, state, or local level, it is likely to closely resemble the CSF Fund program in its basic design.[4]

Apart from its similarity to proposals for publicly funded vouchers, other features of the CSF program make it well suited for empirical study. It is the largest voucher program in the United States, serving approximately 40,000 students, and it is national in scope, thereby increasing confidence that any findings concerning selection are not simply a reflection of the special characteristics of a particular locality. Moreover, because the number of eligible applicants far exceeded the number of available scholarships, recipients were selected by lottery, which means families were assigned randomly to test and control groups. Portions of our analysis take advantage of the random assignment of families to treatment and control conditions.

PREVIOUS RESEARCH

Existing research on the question of who would be most likely to use vouchers is relatively limited. Some scholars have inferred the extent of the impact of vouchers from data on current public and private school enrollments. This research has found that families with higher incomes and more education are more likely to send their children to a private

---

[3]T. M. Moe, *Schools, Vouchers, and the American Public* (Washington, D.C.: Brookings Institution Press, 2001), chap. 9.

[4]Moe's study also demonstrates that Americans favor imposing certain limited regulations on private schools with regard to curriculum, academic performance, and admissions policies. To the extent that the CSF places no additional restrictions on participating private schools apart from existing state regulations, it is somewhat out of step with national public opinion on this one issue. However, because such measures would likely serve to ameliorate any detrimental consequences a voucher system might have on educational segregation, a study of the CSF simply represents a particularly stringent test for vouchers.

school.[5] The relative importance of these two factors, however, has been difficult to establish. These studies have also found that parents are more likely to go private when the perceived or actual performance of their local public schools is low, suggesting that they are motivated at least in part by academic quality.[6] Religious commitment, too, appears to be an important factor in increasing the appeal of private schooling, although limitations in the data that are available have precluded comprehensive analysis of this issue. Still, it is quite clear that Catholic families are more likely to select private schools.[7]

The findings of this line of research regarding the extent to which considerations of race motivate private school enrollment have been less conclusive. Although blacks, Hispanics, and immigrants are substantially less likely to attend private schools than native-born whites, 70 percent of the variation can be accounted for by differences in parental income and education.[8] The extent to which the remaining differences are due to a desire to attend ethnically heterogeneous schools has not been conclusively determined.

Although informative, studies of public and private school attendance are limited by the fact that their inferences are based on the observation of enrollment decisions made under current policies; specifically, they do not tell us much about what would happen if vouchers substantially reduced the cost of a private education. To obtain a better estimate of the likely consequences of a voucher system, Moe asked parents whether they would be interested in sending their child

[5]See: J. E. Long and E. F. Toma, "The Determinants of Private School Attendance, 1970–80," *Review of Economics and Statistics* 70 (1988): 351–57; R. J. Buddin and J. J. Cordes, "School Choice in California: Who Chooses Private Schools?" *Journal of Urban Economics* 44 (1998): 110–34; J. R. Betts and R. W. Fairlie, "Explaining Ethnic, Racial, and Immigrant Differences in Private School Attendance," *Journal of Urban Economics* 50 (2001): 26–51.

[6]R. H. Lankford and J. H. Wyckoff, "Primary and Secondary School Choice Among Public and Religious Alternatives," *Economics of Education Review* 11 (1992): 311–37; Buddin and Cordes.

[7]See Long and Toma; Buddin and Cordes.

[8]Betts and Fairlie.

to a private or a parochial school if they could afford it. His results suggest that the appeal of private education is actually strongest among parents who are of minority background, of low income, and dissatisfied with the academic quality of their child's current school. Among less advantaged families, it is those who are better educated who are most likely to say they would go private if they could afford it.[9]

Data from the CSF survey allow us to see whether parental responses to Moe's survey are consistent with those obtained when vouchers are actually made available. By looking at the CSF data, we can infer the effects of vouchers from parents' revealed preferences regarding their children's education, when a voucher lowers the cost to the family of private schooling. The data also provide information on the success of voucher applicants in obtaining access to a private school. As Moe acknowledges, there is a substantial difference between expressing an interest in private education and successfully enrolling in a private school. In short, the CSF data provide information not only on selection that may occur as the result of differences in parental assiduousness in pursuing a voucher opportunity, but also on selection that may occur as the result of the actions of private school administrators, who might discriminate against minority and poor families.

DATA COLLECTION PROCEDURES

To ascertain the potential effects of vouchers on the composition of public and private schools, we provide estimates of the characteristics of those who applied for school vouchers when they were made available and estimates of the characteristics of those who used a voucher when it was offered to them. To provide these estimates, we rely upon two sources of data. First, the Program on Education Policy and Governance at Harvard University (PEPG) conducted a telephone survey of 2,368 CSF applicants with children enrolled in

---

[9]Moe, chap. 5.

public school, in grades 1 through 8, randomly sampled from the universe of applicants whose eligibility had been confirmed.[10] Applicants were surveyed in the summer following the first school year after CSF scholarships were awarded (June–August 2000). The sample was drawn to match the overall geographic distribution of CSF applicants. One parent in each family and those children in grades 4 and above were interviewed. Because the survey was specifically designed to gauge the experiences of those who switched from public to private schools, in addition to a battery of standard demographic questions, respondents were also asked about their attitudes toward their schools.

To make possible a comparison of the sample of applicants with a sample of the eligible population at large, PEPG administered a similar survey to a cross-section of families who meet the CSF program's eligibility criteria. These were defined as families with children in grades 1 through 8, who have low-to-moderate incomes (less than $40,000), and live in cities with a population of 200,000 or more. When compared with the actual criteria used by the CSF, this definition is close but not exact. Inasmuch as families could have an annual household income of up to 270 percent of the federally defined poverty line and still qualify for a voucher, our definition sets a lower income bound, making the differences between applicants and the eligible population reported below appear larger than they may have been in reality. The same survey was also administered to a national probability sample of all households with children in grades 1 through 8.

---

[10]The survey was administered by Taylor Nelson Sofres Intersearch, a professional survey research firm. According to the guidelines of the American Association for Public Opinion Research, *Standard Definitions: Final Dispositions of Case Codes and Outcome Rates for Surveys* (Ann Arbor, Mich., 2000), the adjusted response rate is 46 percent. As detailed in AAPOR's guidelines, this response rate uses as its denominator an estimate of the percentage of eligible cases among the unknown cases. We generated that estimate by assuming that the percentage of ineligible households among those we interviewed is the same as the percentage among those we did not interview (43%).

These cross-sectional surveys were given to members of a panel assembled by Knowledge Networks, Inc., and administered over Web TV, a device that connects one's television to the Internet. In spite of the two different modes of survey administration, we are reasonably confident that data from the two sources can be compared. Knowledge Networks' panel is constructed using a probability sample of the U.S. population who are initially contacted by telephone, and data are weighted to account for nonresponse (either to the initial invitation to join the panel or the request to complete this particular survey). Moreover, comparisons of results from conventional RDD telephone and Knowledge Networks surveys show them to be substantively similar.[11]

Our survey of CSF applicants means that we have extensive data on applicants to the largest operating voucher program, private or public, in the United States. Coupling this information with our cross-sectional survey of the eligible population enables us to compare the profile of applicant and nonapplicant families, and in that way to determine who chooses to apply for a school voucher. The survey administered to CSF applicants also allows us to assess the characteristics of those who use a voucher when it is offered. Recall that CSF awards its vouchers randomly, so we need not worry about systematic differences between families offered a voucher and those who did not receive an offer.[12] Therefore, simply restricting our analysis to the families in our sample who won the lottery allows us to identify the determinants of voucher take-up among those who applied for the program.

We should note that although the CSF is a national voucher program, it was not advertised uniformly across the United States. The program received invaluable national publicity when Oprah Winfrey mentioned it on her popular television

---

[11]See R. P. Berrens, A. K. Bohura, et al., *The Advent of Internet Surveys for Political Research: A Comparison of Telephone and Internet Samples* (2001).

[12]See Peterson and Campbell.

show, but for the most part CSF program operators advertised through local channels. The extent to which the CSF was advertised more in one type of community than another is likely to affect the demographic profile of our applicant sample. For example, it is possible that African Americans applied more frequently in part because the voucher program was advertised more heavily in areas where African Americans lived. Similarly, Latinos may have been less likely to apply, because the voucher program did not advertise as heavily in those parts of the country (notably the West) where Latinos are concentrated. Research is under way to determine the extent to which CSF's advertising affected the composition of the applicant pool.

WHO CHOOSES TO APPLY FOR VOUCHERS? COMPARING APPLICANTS WITH THE ELIGIBLE POPULATION

Table 1 provides a straightforward comparison of the demographic characteristics of voucher applicants with a national sample of public school families who meet the voucher program's income eligibility requirements.[13] When compared with the total population eligible for the program, voucher applicants appear modestly advantaged, indicating that the voucher program "skims" the more desirable families among the population eligible for vouchers. The skimming is quite modest, however, and may be due in part to the fact that our definition of the eligible population was somewhat more restrictive than the program's own guidelines.

Some differences were statistically insignificant or so small that they hardly justify the skimming metaphor. Twenty-three percent of the mothers of voucher applicants reported that they had a college degree, as compared with 20 percent of eligible public school families. Students applying for

---

[13]In the remainder of this chapter we identify the CSF program, its applicants, and its users, as simply the voucher program, voucher applicants, and voucher users.

TABLE 1

Demographic Background of Voucher Applicants
and Those in Eligible Population

	Voucher Applicants	National Sample of Voucher-Eligible Public School Families
Mother graduated from college	23%	20%[b]
Live in two-parent household	52%	46%[c]
Mother's age (average)	37.1	37.2
Mother born in U.S.A.	82%	83%
Lived in current residence ≥ 2 yrs.	81%	71%[c]
Black	49%	26%[c]
Hispanic	17%	25%[c]
Catholic	25%	28%[b]
Attend church at least 1/week	66%	38%[c]
Number	2303–2368	874–971

[a]Significant at 10%; [b]significant at 5%; [c]significant at 1%.

Note: Data from national sample are weighted to ensure representativeness. Sample of applicants not offered a voucher.

voucher scholarships were also only slightly more likely than the eligible population to live with both parents. Nor were there any significant differences between the two groups in terms of the average age of the child's mother or the percentage of mothers who had been born in the United States. However, applicant families were 10 percentage points more likely than the eligible population as a whole to have lived in their current residence for two years.

The largest differences between these two groups of families involved their racial composition. Whereas 26 percent of the eligible population was African American, no less than 49 percent of voucher applicants were. By contrast, Betts and Fairlie found disproportionately low private school attendance rates among blacks; however, Moe found that minority families were particularly interested in moving their children from public to private schools.[14] When interpreting this result it is important to recall our earlier caveat that at this point we are unable to determine the extent to which the large proportion of blacks among CSF applicants is a function of CFS's marketing strategy. Nevertheless, it seems safe to conclude that the demand for vouchers among African Americans is larger than one would assume if one looked only at patterns of private school usage in the absence of an external subsidy.

Given the large network of relatively inexpensive Catholic private schools and the propensity of Catholic families to send their children to parochial schools, it is somewhat surprising that voucher applicants were actually slightly less likely to be Catholic than the eligible population. Nevertheless, religiously observant families were more likely to apply for a voucher than the less observant. Sixty-six percent of voucher applicants reported that they attend church at least once a week, a response given by only 38 percent of eligible public-school families.

Table 2 provides information on the level of parental involvement in school on the part of applicants, as compared with the eligible population.[15] In some ways, applicants seem more involved with their public schools; in other ways, less so. On the one hand, voucher applicants report having attended more parent-teacher conferences during the past year than did the parents in the eligible population, and they

_____

[14]See Betts and Fairlie; Moe.

[15]The sample size for applicants is smaller for the portions of the analysis that address parental involvement with school, parental satisfaction with school, and parental reports of public school characteristics, because relevant data on these issues were available only for that portion of the applicant sample who were not offered a voucher. Because our survey was administered one year after lottery winners received their vouchers, their answers would reflect their experiences after switching schools, not their experiences with their public schools at the time that they applied to CSF. Fifteen percent of the control-group families in our sample who did not receive a scholarship nevertheless enrolled their children in a private school and have also been excluded form the analysis. Although the latter exclusion involves a departure from the random assignment research design, including them in the analysis does not change any of the substantive results reported in Tables 2, 3, or 4. Because the families in the control group were randomly selected from the total set of applicants, these results may be generalized to the total population.

TABLE 2

Parental Involvement of Voucher Applicants and Those in Eligible Population

	Voucher Applicants	National Sample of Voucher-Eligible Public-School Families
PT conferences per year	3.1	2.5[c]
Telephone conversations per year	2.4	2.7[c]
Volunteered in school (4-point scale)	0.9	0.7[c]
Talk to other parents (4-point scale)	1.9	1.9
Number	662–669	964–968

[c]Significant at 1%.

Note: Data from national sample are weighted to ensure representativeness. Sample of applicants not offered a voucher.

also report that they were more likely to volunteer in their child's school than did the other group of parents. On the other hand, applicants for the program spoke less frequently with their child's teacher by phone.[16]

One way of reconciling these findings is to distinguish between teacher-initiated involvement and parent-initiated involvement with the school. Taking advantage of parent-teacher conferences and volunteering at school may come at the initiative of parents, and our data suggest that parents who make the effort to participate in school life in this way are also the ones who apply for vouchers. Phone conversations with teachers, on the other hand, may originate at the school. Our results indicate that when a school does not communicate effectively with its families, they are more likely to apply for a voucher.

---

[16]Specific questions are: (1) "How many parent-teacher conferences did you or someone else attend for [child's name] this school year?" (2) "How many times did you or someone else speak with [child's name] principal or teacher on the telephone this school year?" (3) "About how many hours have you or someone else volunteered in [child's name] school this past month? Is it none, one to two hours, three to five hours, or six or more hours?" (4) "How often do you or someone else talk with families who have children at [child's name] school? Would you say very often, often, not very often, or never?"

The decision to apply for a voucher may be influenced by a student's academic ability or rate of progress in school. Our survey data do not have precise evidence on a student's academic ability such as might be gained from the administration of a nationally normed examination. However, parents were asked whether their child had ever been diagnosed as having a learning disability. As Table 3 indicates, there was no measurable difference between the percentage of students applying for the program and the eligible population who had been so diagnosed.

The survey responses of students in grades 4 through 8 provide further insight into the academic experiences of students in families who applied for a scholarship. As also can be seen in Table 3, students whose families applied for a voucher reported that they expected to stay in school longer than did students among the eligible population as a whole. However, a higher percentage of applicant students than those in the eligible population agreed that they would read better with more help. Students were also asked whether or not their schoolwork was difficult and if they were having trouble keeping up in school.[17] When responses to the two items were combined into a standardized index of school difficulty, the comparison suggests that voucher applicants, on average, considered their schoolwork to be less challenging than the eligible population.[18] In general, then, this pattern of results suggests that the families most likely to apply for a scholarship were those with students who are academically ambitious and frustrated with their progress.

---

[17]The specific questions are: (1) "How far in school do you intend to go: probably won't graduate from high school, will go to college but might not graduate, will graduate from college, will go to more school after college"; (2) "How strongly do you agree or disagree with the following statements? Do you strongly agree, somewhat agree, somewhat disagree, or strongly disagree?": Class work was hard to learn; I had trouble keeping up with the homework; I would read much better if I had more help.

[18]The index is additive, with the two measures simply summed. That total was then divided by its standard deviation, thus producing an index with a standard deviation of 1.

TABLE 3

Student Academic Characteristics of Voucher
Applicants and Those in Eligible Population

	Voucher Applicants	National Sample of Voucher-Eligible Public School Families
Parental Reports		
Student has been diagnosed with a learning disability	14%	13%
Number	692	943
Student Reports		
How far student will go in school (5-point scale)	4.1	3.8[c]
Would read better with help (4-point scale)	2.6	2.4[b]
Class work is hard (4-point scale)	2.1	2.3
Trouble keeping up (4-point scale)	2.1	2.2
Difficulty in school index (varies between 1 and 3)	2.1	2.6[c]
Number	223–36	482–526

[b]Significant at 5%; [c]significant at 1%.

Note: Data from national sample are weighted to ensure representativeness. Sample of applicants not offered a voucher.

The largest and most consistent differences between applicants for the voucher program and the eligible population appear in their level of satisfaction with the public schools their children were attending. As is evident in Table 4, the parents of voucher applicants were far less satisfied with their schools than were eligible nonapplicants, suggesting that voucher applicants were motivated largely by considerations of academic quality. Nor were these differences in satisfaction simply a function of gross disparities in the resources available in respondents' schools, at least as measured by class size. Voucher applicants' classes were, on average, no larger than those of eligible nonapplicants. Interestingly, however, the public schools attended by applicants were approximately fifty students larger than the schools attended by students in the eligible sample.

Table 5 addresses the concern that significant numbers of parents would use vouchers to remove their children from schools that are attended by large numbers of minorities, thus increasing racial segregation. Each row reports the percentage of families whose children attend schools whose racial composition is at least 90 percent, first for blacks, then Hispanics, then whites. A little less than half of black CSF applicants attend schools that are 90 percent minority, compared with only 32 percent of blacks in the national cross-section. For Hispanics, both percentages were 23 percent. When the same

TABLE 4

Parental Satisfaction and School Characteristics of
Voucher Applicants and Those in Eligible Population

	Voucher Applicants	National Sample of Voucher-Eligible Public School Families
Percent "very satisfied" with:		
Academic quality	24%	38%[c]
Safety	22%	38%[c]
Location	32%	51%[c]
Discipline	22%	33%[c]
Teaching of values	26%	36%[c]
School Satisfaction Index	5.0	5.5[c]
Parent's grade for school (4-point scale)	2.6	2.9[c]
Class size (average)	24	24
School size (average)	500	450[c]
Number	575–695	700–965

[c]Significant at 1%.

Note: Data from national sample are weighted to ensure representativeness. Sample of applicants not offered a voucher.

analysis is restricted to whites, no differences were observed in the percentage of applicants and CSF-eligibles attending schools that are 90 percent minority. Less than 10 percent of whites in both samples attended a school with this demographic profile. Therefore, rather than contributing to "white flight," the CSF scholarship program appears to have substantially increased the educational options available to blacks attending predominantly minority schools.

WHO USES A SCHOLARSHIP WHEN OFFERED? MODELING VOUCHER TAKE-UP

To model the decision to use a voucher among those families who won the lottery and were thus offered a voucher, we constructed a dichotomous dependent variable that equals 1 if the family used the voucher and equals 0 if they did not. Our models include a number of factors that past research on vouchers and other targeted social benefits has suggested may

TABLE 5

Racial Composition of Schools Attended by
Voucher Applicants and Those in Eligible Population

	Voucher Applicants	National Sample of Voucher-Eligible Public School Families
	(Percentage attending 90% or more minority school)	(Percentage attending 90% or more minority school)
Blacks	47%	32%[c]
Number	359	205
Hispanics	23%	23%
Number	111	186
Whites	8%	8%
Number	146	446

[c]Significant at 1%.

Note: Data from national sample are weighted to ensure representativeness. Sample of applicants not offered a voucher.

influence voucher take-up. Note that questions pertaining to individual parents were asked in regard to the mother or female guardian in the home (except in the extremely rare situation where there was only a father or male guardian in the home, in which case questions were asked about him). This decision reflects the fact that research has shown that attributes of the mother are the better predictor of academic attainment.[19] Although we use the term "mother" to simplify the discussion, such references should be taken to mean "mother or female guardian."

Two variables were included indicating the level of educational attainment by the mother: whether or not she was a college graduate, and whether or not she had attended some college, both as distinct from having received no more than a high school diploma.[20] These variables provide information on the extent to which more educated parents are more likely to use a voucher, as well as on whether private schools give priority to children from better-educated families. In addition, a measure of the mother's age is included in the model, with the expectation that younger mothers, particularly those who had children while in their teens, might be less able or less motivated to enter the private school market. Because past research has suggested that most immigrant groups are less likely to send their children to private schools,[21] we add another variable indicating whether or not the mother was born in the United States. We also include a measure of the mother's labor-force participation, since it has been suggested that "holding family income constant, a family will be less wealthy in real terms if both parents must work to earn that family income, since the family must forgo the mother's household production."[22]

---

[19]C. Jencks, *Who Gets Ahead? The Determinants of Economic Success in America* (New York: Basic Books, 1979).

[20]The small number of mothers reporting that they have a graduate degree were combined with those with a bachelor's degree.

[21]See Betts and Fairlie.

[22]Buddin and Cordes, p. 125.

We also include in the model a dichotomous variable indicating whether or not the student lives in a home with two parents, on the assumption that two-parent homes will have more resources to devote to seeking out and enrolling in a private school as well as to fulfilling any additional responsibilities that might come from having a child attend a school in the private sector. Yet another variable accounts for whether the family has lived in its current residence for two or more years. The longer a family lives in a community, the more likely they are to be informed about the full range of educational options available to them. Moreover, evidence from studies of other means-tested social benefits suggests that the families most likely to complete the administrative tasks associated with enrolling are those who expect to be eligible for an extended period of time.[23] Given that switching a child from public to private school constitutes a major commitment for the child and the family, more transient families might be less willing to make this investment.

Moe's research suggests that black families living in the north are more interested in moving their children to private schools than are other racial or ethnic groups, although the same is not true of Southern blacks.[24] Consequently, we include in the model a term for blacks in Southern states (defined as the states of the former Confederacy), and another for blacks residing in the North (more accurately but clumsily, the rest of the United States). Similarly, we account for whether the mother identifies as Hispanic.

Because an overwhelming percentage of private schools in the United States have a religious affiliation, the debate over school vouchers is often a thinly cloaked debate over what constitutes an appropriate—and constitutional—relationship between church and state. Given that Catholic parochial schools constitute a large proportion of the nation's private

---

[23]B. P. McCall, "The Impact of Unemployment Benefit Levels on Recipiency," *Journal of Business and Economic Statistics* 13 (1995): 189–98; R. M. Blank and P. Ruggles, "When Do Women Use Aid to Families with Dependent Children and Food Stamps?" *Journal of Human Resources* 31 (1996): 57–89.

[24]Moe, chap. 5.

schools, the model also includes a term indicating whether the family is Catholic, as well as an interaction term between Catholic religious affiliation and frequency of church attendance. The interaction allows us to distinguish between nominal Catholics and those who are religiously observant. Schools founded by fundamentalist and evangelical Christians constitute a large, and the fastest growing, segment of the private school market, and so we include an indicator of whether the mother is a "born-again" Christian. For the same reasons, we also include a measure of the frequency with which the mother attends religious services. Because the assertion that one is a "born-again" Christian is itself a measure of religious orthodoxy, we would not expect its interaction with church attendance to be a significant factor, an expectation borne out in model specifications not shown here. For parsimony's sake, we therefore do not include it here.

A common concern raised about school vouchers is that private schools will turn away students with learning disabilities, leaving these high-needs children as a larger proportion of the public school population.[25] We thus also include a variable indicating whether or not a family has a child with a learning disability.

We include measures of both the family's income and the number of children in the family.[26] Research on higher education has shown that parental willingness to support financially their children's education is strongly related to their household income and family size.[27] However, these two factors together also determine the value of the voucher offered by CSF, or what is effectively the discount they would receive on the price

---

[25]L. F. Rothstein, "School Choice and Students with Disabilities," in S. D. Sugarman and F. R. Kemerer, eds., *School Choice and Social Controversy* (Washington, D.C.: Brookings Institution Press, 1997), p. 357.

[26]This income measure is different from the one used in the comparison between voucher applicants and a cross-section of the eligible population. Previously, we reported income as reported in our telephone survey, using a closed-choice survey question. Here we use applicants' income as they reported it to CSF for verification.

[27]L. C. Steelman and B. Powell, "Sponsoring the Next Generation: Parental Willingness to Pay for Higher Education," *American Journal of Sociology* 96 (1991): 1505–29.

of private school tuition. If the CSF formula for determining a family's tuition discount is calibrated precisely to the family's ability to pay, then neither of these variables should have a statistically significant effect on take-up.

Finally, we also account for two factors describing the context of the communities in which applicants live. First, we have calculated the size of the private school market in a respondent's metropolitan area. While most of the discussion of "who uses" has centered on the characteristics of individuals, it seems plausible that the availability of private schools within one's community is also a major determinant of whether a family chooses to go private. Private school market share is operationalized as the percentage of elementary and secondary school students attending private school within a family's metropolitan statistical area (MSA), as reported in the 1990 U.S. Census. Second, we also include a measure of the racial composition of a family's local public schools, operationalized as the percentage of African American students in the elementary and secondary schools within a respondent's zip code. These data are again taken from the 1990 U.S. Census. We use zip code as the level of aggregation for this measure because it most closely reflects the racial composition of the public schools in a respondent's neighborhood. By including this measure, we are able to test whether vouchers facilitate racial segregation in the public schools. That is, do families use vouchers to flee predominantly African American schools?

Table 6 presents a simple comparison between users and decliners on all items included in the logistic model presented in Table 7, with an indication of whether the simple difference between the two groups is statistically significant. Voucher users are less likely to have attended "some college," but more likely to have graduated from college. A smaller percentage of mothers in families that opt to use a voucher work full time, while a higher proportion of these families have lived in their current residence for at least two years. There are also smaller percentages of Southern blacks and Hispanics among voucher users, and higher percentages of Catholics and frequent church attenders. The income of users is modestly higher than that of decliners, and their families are slightly smaller. Users have a slightly smaller private school market than decliners. Interestingly, users also have a lower percentage of African Americans in their local schools, contrary to the fear that vouchers are a means for families to flee predominantly minority schools.

Logistic regression is used as the estimator in the multivariate analysis, because the dependent variable is dichotomous.

TABLE 6
Characteristics of Voucher Users and Decliners

	Decliners	Users
Attended "some college"	43%	37%[b]
College graduate	23%	30%[c]
Mother's age	37	37
Mother born in U.S.A.	82%	85%
Mother works full time	60%	51%[c]
Two-parent household	53%	54%
Lived in current residence ≥ 2 yrs.	79%	86%[c]
Black, Northern states	28%	26%
Black, Southern states	23%	13%[c]
Hispanic	17%	13%[b]
Catholic	24%	31%[c]
"Born-again" Christian	41%	39%
Attend religious services 1/week or more	65%	74%[c]
Child has learning disability	14%	12%
Family income	$22,110	$23,854[c]
Number of children (average)	1.75	1.62[c]
Private school share of market	12%	13%[c]
Local schools' racial composition (% black)	38%	33%[c]
Number	1,146–1,187	469–492

[b]Significant at 5%; [c]significant at 1%.

Note: All figures are percentages unless otherwise indicated.

TABLE 7
Logistic Regression Results for Voucher Usage

	Standard Model		Whites Only	
Attended "some college"	-0.292^a	(0.152)	-0.038	(0.284)
College graduate	0.140	(0.167)	0.622^b	(0.309)
Mother's age	-0.020^b	(0.009)	-0.029	(0.018)
Mother born in U.S.A.	0.327	(0.206)	0.854	(0.692)
Mother works full time	-0.134	(0.133)	-0.185	(0.238)
Two-parent household	-0.353^b	(0.141)	-0.543^a	(0.278)
Lived in current residence $\geq$ 2 yrs.	0.473^c	(0.177)	0.870^c	(0.335)
Black, Northern states	-0.570^c	(0.194)		
Black, Southern states	-0.973^c	(0.221)		
Hispanic	-0.692^c	(0.234)		
Catholic	0.108	(0.270)	0.743^a	(0.433)
Catholic church attendance	0.626^b	(0.306)	0.264	(0.525)
"Born again" Christian	0.232	(0.160)	0.819^b	(0.323)
Church attendance	0.382^b	(0.178)	0.587^a	(0.349)
Child has learning disability	-0.368^a	(0.206)	-0.352	(0.341)
Family income	0.078	(0.054)	0.239^b	(0.100)
Number of children	-0.246^c	(0.079)	-0.109	(0.144)
Private school share of market	5.078^c	(1.485)	6.369^b	(2.839)
Local schools' racial composition	-0.093	(0.243)	0.119	(0.582)
Constant	-0.881^a	(0.496)	-2.682^b	(1.085)
Number	1,377		370	
Pseudo-R^2	.07		.11	
Naïve prediction	70.7		56.8	
% model correctly predicted	72.8		68.11	

[a]Significant at 10%; [b]significant at 5%; [c]significant at 1%.
Note: Standard errors are given in parentheses.

Column 1 of Table 7 displays the results of a model with all the variables just described. Perhaps the first thing to note is that the model itself does a relatively poor job of explaining "who uses." The model's improvement over a naïve prediction is minimal, and the pseudo-R^2 is relatively low. We can thus conclude that the determinants of voucher usage are outside the numerous demographic variables included in this model.

Among the variables included in the model, there are a few surprises. Attending "some college" is actually a negative predictor of using a voucher (remember that this is relative to having a high school education or less), while having a college degree is not statistically significant. It does not appear, therefore, that, *ceteris paribus*, the pool of voucher users is more educated than decliners. This inference is confirmed by results from a model specification not shown in which the effects of mother's educational attainment, as estimated by a single ordinal variable, are once again so small as to be statistically insignificant.

Mother's age is a significant factor in determining who uses vouchers, but in the opposite direction from that predicted. Rather than younger mothers being less likely to use vouchers, they are more likely to do so. Families with a foreign-born mother are no less likely to use a voucher; families with a mother who works full time are neither more nor less likely. Surprisingly, families with two parents in the same household are less, not more, likely to take advantage of a voucher.

The measure of residential stability plays a relatively large role in predicting who uses. This means that the families who switch from public to private schools are more established in their communities than those who choose not to make use of a voucher. We hypothesize that this is because they are more aware of private school options for their children. It may also be because "putting down roots" in a neighborhood means that a family is more likely to be embedded in a religious community, many of which may sponsor private schools. Whatever the causal mechanism, it seems clear that under a voucher program, the most residentially mobile families are likely to continue to use the public schools while those who are the least likely to have moved are the most likely to go private.

The coefficient on each of the variables identifying blacks is negative and large, the coefficient for Southern blacks being over twice as large as the one for Northern blacks. These results hold when simply living in the South is entered as a control variable as well. In other words, while African Americans were a disproportionately large percentage of the applicant population, they were less likely to use a voucher, when offered. The results may indicate that private schools are less likely to admit black applicants than white applicants. However, it is also possible that the high percentage of black applicants may indicate that, on average, there was less self-selection, and perhaps less precommitment to using the voucher, on the part of black applicants. If as a consequence the average black family among voucher applicants was less committed to using a voucher upon its offer than a white family, then the take-up rate among African Americans would be lower. One cannot be sure that such an interdependence exists, however, because Hispanics were both less likely to apply for the program than other ethnic groups and less likely to use a voucher when offered one.

Moving to measures of religious affiliation and commitment, simply having a Catholic religious affiliation is not a significant predictor of going private once we also include the interaction between Catholic and church attendance. The coefficient on the interaction term itself, however, is large. Evaluated together, these results suggest that it is not being nominally Catholic that increases a family's likelihood of switching from the public to private sector, but being a practicing Catholic. Similarly, simply identifying as a born-again Christian has no measurable effect on voucher take-up, although frequency of church attendance does. In sum, it appears as though religious families, particularly practicing Catholics, are more likely to use vouchers. For Catholics and non-Catholics alike, frequency of church attendance predicts voucher take-up; nominal religious identifications, however, are unimportant.

The coefficient for learning disability is negative and statistically significant at the 0.10 level. Therefore we can cautiously suggest that families with children who are learning disabled may be less likely to use a voucher.

Income is not a statistically significant factor determining who uses vouchers, which is exactly what CSF program operators intended in their design of the program. However, the number of children in a family is negatively related to the decision to use a voucher. This is almost certainly due to the fact that even though CSF attempts to account for the number of children in a family when determining voucher amounts, more children nonetheless means that more tuition is due.

The size of the private school market is positive and highly significant, meaning that "who uses" is largely determined by where opportunities to enroll in private schools can be found. However, the measure of the local schools' racial composition does not approach statistical significance, indicating that families in general are not more likely to use vouchers as a function of their local schools' racial composition.

One might still object that this is not a full test of white flight hypothesis, because the relevant question is really whether *whites* consider the racial composition of their neighborhood's public schools when deciding to use a voucher. Column 2 reports the results of the same model as in Column 1, but restricted to whites only. Again, we see that the coefficient for schools' racial composition cannot be distinguished from 0. In sum, we can find no evidence that vouchers contribute to racial segregation.

Because the coefficients in Table 7 are from logistic regression models, the relative magnitude of their effects is not intuitively interpretable. In order to compare their substantive impact, Figure 1 displays the first differences of each variable as generated with Monte Carlo simulation.[28] With all other variables set to their means, we generate the change in the

---

[28]M. Tomz, J. Wittenburg, et al., CLARIFY: Software for interpreting and presenting statistical results, Cambridge, Mass., 2001.

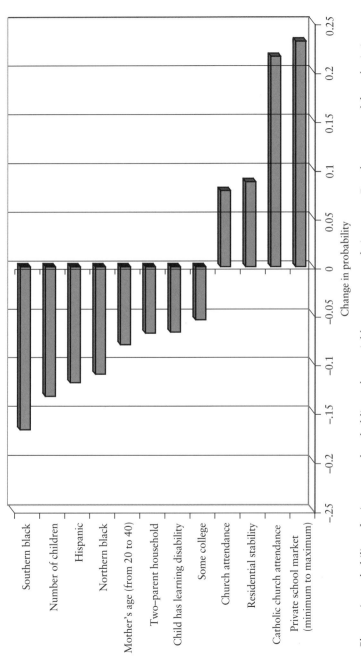

Change in probability of using a voucher, holding other variables constant at their means. Results generated from logistic regression coefficients reported in Table 7.

FIGURE 1. Comparison of the Impact of Different Variables on the Decision to Use a Voucher

predicted probability of using a voucher as each successive variable has its value vary from the minimum to the maximum.[29]

This figure reveals that private school market share and the interaction between Catholic religious affiliation and church attendance have the largest substantive impacts of all the variables in the model. The increase in the probability of using a voucher rises by 0.23 from the MSA with the smallest private school market to the one with the largest. This effect is statistically indistinguishable from the Catholic church attendance interaction, which has an impact of 0.22 (varying the interaction term as well as Catholic and church attendance individually). Of the factors that decrease the likelihood of using a voucher, the one with the largest impact is being an African American in the South, which *ceteris paribus* results in a drop of 0.17 in the predicted probability of voucher take-up. In light of the concern over the fate of learning-disabled children under a school voucher system, note also that having a child with a learning disability has one of the smallest negative impacts in the model.

DO PRIVATE SCHOOLS SKIM THE CREAM OF THE CROP? WHY CHILDREN ARE NOT ADMITTED TO THE SCHOOL OF THEIR CHOICE

We have noted that the size of the private school market in a family's community is a significant predictor of whether a family goes private. In other words, the number of local private schools is an important factor in determining voucher take-up. However, there is another way that private school availability might affect this decision. Private schools can be as selective as they wish, and it could be that children have difficulty gaining admission to the private school of their choice because of poor academic performance. On the other

---

[29] The only exception was for mother's age, which we do not allow to vary across the entire range because of a few extreme outliers; instead it varies from 20 to 40, a reasonable range.

hand, existing research on Catholic schools—the most common type of school attended by voucher recipients—has shown that they are generally not selective in their admissions, not even with regard to religion.[30]

As Table 8 shows, 38 percent of the families who were offered a voucher but declined it reported that they did not gain admission to their preferred school. Although this is not necessarily the sole reason that they did not use the voucher, presumably it is a significant factor in deciding whether or not to enroll in a private school. Given that only a little more than a third of decliner parents say that their child was not admitted to their preferred school, it would appear that difficulty in gaining admission to a private

TABLE 8

Reasons Decliners Gave for Not Gaining
Admission to a Preferred School

Percentage of Voucher Decliners Not Admitted to a Preferred School	38.1%
Number	1,165
Cited as the reason child was not admitted to preferred school	
Could not afford	45%
"Child had to attend neighborhood school"	14%
No space available	10%
Transportation problems	8%
Moved away from school	3%
Admissions test	3%
Other reason	18%
Total	101%
Number	440

Note: Percentages do not add to 100 because of rounding.

---

[30]A. S. Bryk, V. Lee, and P. Holland, *Catholic Schools and the Common Good* (Cambridge, Mass.: Harvard University Press, 1993).

school is not the primary factor in deciding whether or not to use a voucher.

Each parent who reported that her child did not gain admission to the family's school of choice was also asked to identify the reason why from a list we provided. In reading the results as displayed in Table 8, keep in mind that the percentages are of those parents whose child did not gain admission to the school they wanted. The percentages would be considerably smaller if we used all decliners, or all those offered a voucher, as the denominators. By far the most common explanation parents gave for not gaining admission to a preferred school is that they could not afford it; almost half (45 percent) mentioned this as the reason. As already noted, even with a voucher private school tuition can be too costly, especially for low-income families.

Contrary to the concern that private schools will accept only the most academically proficient students from the public schools, only 3 percent of these parents reported that their child was not admitted because of an admissions test. This is the same percentage whose children did not end up in their preferred school because the family moved. Fourteen percent chose the statement that "their child had to attend a neighborhood school," which was included on the list as a default explanation for those parents who do not have a clearly articulated reason why their child did not end up in a preferred school. Similarly, 18 percent said that there was another reason why their child was not admitted; clearly future research needs to explore further what these reasons might be because these two categories equal almost a third of parents whose children were not admitted to their first-choice school.

Ten percent said that there was no space at their preferred school—again a reminder that the supply of private schools is an important component in the capacity of families to take advantage of the offer of a voucher. Eight percent said that transportation problems were the reason, a surprisingly low percentage given that many private schools do not provide students with transportation to and from school.

There are two forces shaping the contours of the private school population. One might be thought of as the demand for private education; it has been modeled here by examining characteristics of families who go private when offered a voucher. The other force is on the supply side: the availability of private schools. Based on our analysis, we conclude that in one respect supply matters greatly, and in another it matters little. As already noted, the overall size of the private school market in a metropolitan area is a critical factor in determining voucher take-up rate, yet the private schools to which voucher applicants wish to send their children do not appear to be terribly selective. At the very least, they do not seem to select only high-performing students.

To the extent that there is a single explanation for non-admission to a family's preferred school, it would appear to be the cost of attending a private school. However, even this reason is selected by only 45 percent of parents whose children are not in their first-choice school. As a percentage of all families offered a voucher, this means that only 12 percent could not afford their preferred school.[31] And presumably even this percentage would grow smaller if the size of the vouchers were increased to more closely approximate the full cost of private school tuition.

CONCLUSION: ESTIMATING IMPACTS OF VOUCHERS ON PUBLIC AND PRIVATE SCHOOLS

The market simulations that Moe conducted led him to conclude that one of the most significant consequences of the implementation of a large-scale voucher system would be a dramatic overall reduction in the differences in social composition between the public and private sectors that

---

[31]That is, of all families who won the lottery, 12 percent reported that they could not afford their preferred school.

exist under current policies. As he puts it: "While we cannot know exactly how many parents will actually go private when given the choice, the direction of change is toward very substantial moderation of existing social biases and a considerable closing of the existing social gaps between public and private."[32] In particular, racial disparities between the two sectors would be reduced. Moe's estimates are interesting, but they rely upon parents' statements regarding their likely behavior under hypothetical conditions. His estimates, moreover, do not take into account any selection that may occur as a result of the decisions taken by private schools. In this final section, we combine information on CSF users with data from our national probability sample of all families with children in grades 1 through 8 in order to provide another estimate of the effects of a voucher program on the composition of the public and private educational sectors. For the most part, the estimates are similar to those reported by Moe.

Table 9 displays the estimated effects. In 2000, there was a considerable social gap between those attending public and those attending private schools. The differences are particularly large with respect to educational attainment. Over 47 percent of the mothers of students in the private sector report that they have graduated from college, as compared with only 32 percent of public school mothers. The mothers of private school students are also slightly older than their public school counterparts, and substantially more likely to have been born in the United States, to be Catholic, and to attend church at least once a week. Private school students are significantly less likely than their public school counterparts to be black or Hispanic or to have a learning disability. Surprisingly, the private school students in our sample were somewhat less likely than public school students to live in a two-parent household.

In virtually every respect, the entry of voucher users into the private sector would serve to reduce these biases, often

[32]Moe, p. 164.

TABLE 9

Demographic Characteristics of Voucher
Users and the General Population

	Voucher Users	National Sample of Private School Families	National Sample of Public School Families
Mother graduated from college	30%	47%[c]	32%
Live in two-parent household	54%	57%	63%[c]
Mother born in U.S.A.	85%	93%[c]	87
Mother's age (average)	36.8	39.7[c]	38.3[c]
Lived in current residence ≥ 2 yrs.	86%	79[b]	78%[c]
Black	38%	8%[c]	14%[c]
Hispanic	13%	11%	15%
Catholic	31%	52%[c]	30%
Attend church at least 1/week	74%	62%[c]	36%[c]
Child has learning disability	12%	9%	11%
Number	486–492	260–298	1,716–1,779

[a]Significant at 10%; [b]significant at 5%; [c]significant at 1%.

Note: Data from national sample are weighted to ensure representativeness.

dramatically. With regard to mother's education, for example, not only are voucher users less likely to have a college degree than students currently in private schools, they also have lower levels of educational attainment than public school mothers. The same pattern holds for the percentage of mothers born in the United States, mother's age, and the percentage of students with learning disabilities. A voucher program similar to the CSF program would also reduce the extent to which the private sector overrepresents students from Catholic families.

The impact of a voucher system focused on low-to-moderate income families and publicized in a manner similar to that of the CSF would be particularly striking in the case of racial disparities in private school attendance. Although blacks represent only 8 percent of the students in our sample currently attending private schools, and 14 percent of the public school students, they make up over 38 percent of voucher users. And although the proportion of Hispanics among voucher users is smaller than among public school families nationally, it is still greater than the proportion currently in private schools. Therefore, in spite of the fact that blacks and Hispanics who received vouchers were less likely than white recipients to use them, there is no reason to dispute Moe's claim that "under reasonable assumptions about which parents are most likely to switch sides, the new private sector winds up being more ethnically diverse than the public sector does."[33] Given the fact that private schools in general, and Catholic schools in particular, have been shown to be particularly effective in educating urban minorities, these results are clearly encouraging.[34]

With respect to at least two of the items included in our survey, however, a voucher system with the characteristics of the CSF program might be expected to increase the size of the differences between the public and private sectors. These exceptions underscore once again the importance of religious commitment and residential stability in determining who uses vouchers. Nearly three-quarters of the mothers of students using these vouchers reported that they attend church at least once a week, a percentage even higher than the 62 percent of the mothers of students currently enrolled in private schools. Meanwhile, over 85 percent of voucher users reported that they had lived in their current residence

---

[33]Ibid.

[34]D. Neal, "The Effects of Catholic Secondary Schooling on Educational Attainment," *Journal of Labor Economics* 15 (1997): 98–123; D. N. Figlio and J. A. Stone, "Are Private Schools Really Better?" *Research in Labor Economics* 18 (1999): 115–40.

for more than two years, a response given by 79 percent of current private school parents and 78 percent of those currently attending public schools.

Therefore, with the notable exceptions of religious attendance and residential stability, the entry of voucher families into the private school market would serve to diminish the gap in the social composition of the public and private educational sectors. The effect might be even more substantial if the take-up rate for vouchers could be increased, by increasing either the value of the tuition discount or the amount of information available to low-income parents about private school alternatives. It might also be assumed that the take-up rate would increase naturally over time as more private schools enter the educational market.

Although the CSF is the largest school voucher program in the country and closely resembles proposals made both by policy analysts and by legislators, it is obviously not the same as a large-scale, publicly funded voucher initiative. One must therefore be careful in using our conclusions about the CSF to make generalizations about how school vouchers would work in practice. A publicly funded program would probably be larger in scope and differently advertised to the eligible population. But with that caveat in mind, to the extent that such a program had eligibility requirements resembling those for the CSF and was thus targeted at low-to-moderate income families, our results may speak to the concern that vouchers will "cream" the best students out of the public schools. A one-sentence summary cannot do justice to all our findings, but the evidence suggests that there is little reason to believe that vouchers will simply serve the socially advantaged.

4

A Supply-Side View of Student Selectivity

John E. Chubb

Chief among concerns about school choice is student selectivity, or what is more popularly called "creaming." If parents (or guardians) are allowed to choose the schools their children attend, and schools are required to compete for students and resources, the best students will become concentrated, like rising cream, in the best schools. The weakest students will be left behind in the poorest schools. Educational opportunity, which the public education system is supposed to provide equally to all children, will become even less equal than it is already. Whatever benefits school choice may yield—and they may be considerable for the overall quality of schooling and the level of student achievement—the risks of inequity may simply outweigh them.[1]

On first inspection, selectivity would appear to be an important concern. Some parents are clearly better educated, more knowledgeable about schools, and more interested in their children's education than other parents. More able and interested parents would surely try harder to learn about quality school choices and to make application to those schools. At the same

---

[1]On the theoretical benefits of school choice for student achievement, see esp.: John E. Chubb and Terry M. Moe, *Politics, Markets, and America's Schools* (Washington, D.C.: Brookings Institution Press, 1990).

time, schools would surely prefer to teach children who have interested parents and academic inclinations. Even if schools must accept all students, schools can still orient their programs and recruitment efforts toward the best and the brightest.

History offers some support for this reasoning. For the last half-century, parents have fled the cities for the suburbs, in pursuit of better and safer schools. Private schools proliferated in the South after *Brown v. Board of Education* to serve white families resistant to the integration of public schools. Public magnet schools are often oases of quality, in school systems bereft of decent schools, serving parents shrewd enough or lucky enough to gain admission.[2]

But appearances can be deceiving. The school choice programs being proposed or offered by policymakers today come with safeguards against selectivity.[3] Public opinion surveys indicate that interest in school choice is greatest among poor and minority families, whose children have historically not been the highest achievers.[4] And the simple fact is that experience with school choice is too limited to draw any conclusions confidently about selectivity.[5] History provides

---

[2]For arguments and evidence that school choice promotes inequity and segregation, see: Bruce Fuller, Richard F. Elmore, and Gary Orfield, eds., *Who Chooses? Who Loses? Culture, Institutions, and the Unequal Effects of School Choice* (New York: Teachers College Press, 1996); Ted Fiske and Helen F. Ladd, *When Schools Compete: A Cautionary Tale* (Washington, D.C.: Brookings Institution Press, 2000); and Gary Orfield, *Schools More Separate: Consequences of a Decade of Resegregation* (Cambridge, Mass.: The Civil Rights Project, Harvard University, 2001).

[3]On the importance of the structure of school choice systems, see Moe, Chap. 7 in this volume.

[4]The most comprehensive analysis of public opinion on school choice is Terry M. Moe, *Schools, Vouchers, and the American Public* (Washington, D.C.: Brookings Institution Press, 2001).

[5]The bulk of the empirical evidence on school choice comes from settings that are only proxies for what a widely available, publicly funded system of school choice might look like. The evidence includes especially, on private schools: James S. Coleman, Thomas Hoffer, and Sally Kilgore, *High School Achievement: Public and Private High Schools Compared* (New York: Basic Books, 1982); James S. Coleman and Thomas Hoffer, *Public and Private High Schools: The Impact of Communities* (New York: Basic Books, 1987); and Chubb and Moe, *Politics, Markets, and America's Schools*; on small voucher programs for the economically disadvantaged

evidence of how families with the financial wherewithal have chosen private schools or suburban schools—and how schools have cropped up to meet that demand. But history provides little direct evidence of how families or schools would respond if school choice were made available to parents as a matter of public policy, without regard to financial means.

NEW EVIDENCE

Slowly our knowledge base is improving. In the last decade, policymakers have begun offering parents truly meaningful school choice. Most important, some thirty-seven states now provide for charter schools—public schools largely independent of local school systems and open to all students regardless of achievement, income, or (usually) residence.[6] Charter schools represent a major advance in school choice for two basic reasons. First, and most obviously, they create *demand* for public schools that is not tied to the ability of families to move to new school

students funded through private philanthropy or, in a couple of instances (Milwaukee and Cleveland), public funds: William G. Howell and Paul E. Peterson, *School Choice in Dayton, Ohio: An Evaluation After One Year* (Cambridge, Mass.: Program on Education Policy and Governance, Harvard University, 2000); Paul E. Peterson, William G. Howell, and Jay P. Greene, *An Evaluation of the Cleveland Voucher Program After Two Years* (Program on Educational Policy and Governance, Harvard University, 1999); and Paul E. Peterson, D. Meyers, and William G. Howell, *An Evaluation of the New York City School Scholarships Program: The First Year* (Cambridge, Mass.: Program on Educational Policy and Governance, Harvard University, 1998); on family mobility and competition among public school districts: Caroline M. Hoxby, "Does Competition Among Public Schools Benefit Students and Taxpayers?" *American Economic Review*, 90, no. 5 (December 2000): 1209–38; on family mobility and racial segregation: Orfield, *Schools More Separate*.

[6] On the early experience of charter schools, see: Chester E. Finn, Bruno V. Manno, and Greg Vanourek, *Charter Schools in Action: What Have We Learned?* (Indianapolis: Hudson Institute, 1997); Joe Nathan, *Charter Schools: Creating Hope and Opportunity for American Education* (San Francisco: Jossey-Bass, 1996); and Paul A. Berman et al., *A National Study of Charter Schools, Second-Year Report* (Washington, D.C.: U.S. Department of Education, Office of Educational Research and Improvement, 1998).

districts or to threaten moves to private schools. Prior to charter schools, parents with limited financial means could not demand better or different public schools, except through school board elections and the political process. With the advent of charter schools, all parents have the power to switch schools, creating at least the beginnings of a market for public education.

The second reason charter schools are important is that they create a *supply* of public schools not under the control of local school systems.[7] If parents are given the right to choose among public schools, but all public schools are under the control of a single public authority—that is, the local school system—the right to choose loses much of its force, or certainly the force associated with a market. When the "good choices" are all gone, parents are compelled to send their children to the choices that remain, choices provided by the local school system. Charter schools free the supply of public schools from the traditional sole provider. Charter schools in effect transform a monopoly into a potentially competitive market. Charter schools offer alternatives for families and students, and just as important, incentives for the traditional public schools to change and improve.

The supply of public education is, of course, vital. If parents are free to choose schools, but the schools among which they must choose never change, school choice amounts to little more than a reallocation of educational opportunity. Some students will get to attend better schools, whereas other students will have to attend worse schools. This is not the idea of school choice: the logic of school choice is the logic of the market. Markets require enough suppliers, as well as "buyers," to provide the benefits of competition. If charter schools succeed in creating markets

---

[7]On the general importance of the supply side of school choice, see Paul T. Hill, "The Supply Side of Choice," in Frank Kemmerer and Stephen Sugarman, *School Choice and Social Controversy* (Washington, D.C.: Brookings Institution Press, 2000).

for public schools, they will do so not only through charter schools themselves but also through responses by traditional public schools to the competition.[8] Charter
schools have the potential to stimulate improvement in the
overall quality of schools from which parents choose.

As charter schools, now numbering over 2,000 nationwide, proliferate, and as school systems respond to their
pressure, we have our best opportunity ever to learn how
school choice may affect the selectivity of public schools.
Whom do charter schools attempt to attract? Who chooses
charter schools? How do district schools respond? How do
these new forces of supply and demand seem to affect the
quality and equality of public schools? It may be another
decade before we have confident answers to these questions.
Even the oldest charter schools in America are barely a
decade old,[9] and most states have been authorizing charter
schools for less than a decade. School systems may just be
beginning to compete with charters—instead of suing and
lobbying for them to go away. But the data are beginning to
come in. And they are surprising.

EDISON SCHOOLS INC

Perhaps the largest single source of data on the charter experience is that of Edison Schools Inc, the largest private
manager of public schools in the United States, and also
the largest operator of charter schools. In the fall of 2001,
Edison managed 136 schools in twenty-two states and the
District of Columbia. Located in over fifty communities,
the schools served some 75,000 students. About a third
of the schools were charter schools; the remainder have
schools of choice within public school systems. Edison

---

[8]On the response of public schools to competition, see esp. Caroline M.
Hoxby, Chap 6 this volume.

[9]U.S. Department of Education, *The State of Charter Schools 2000* (Washington, D.C.).

opened its first schools in 1995 and has since increased enrollment at an average rate of about 50 percent per year.[10]

Edison's experience can enlighten both sides of the school choice equation—and in a number of ways. On the demand side, Edison operates scores of public schools of choice, of three distinctly different types: independent charters (with no connection to a local school district), district charters (freed from district management but accountable to a school district), and district schools of choice. Generally, both types of district schools are responses to the competition from independent charters. Who attends the different types of schools?

As the largest private provider of public schools, Edison also offers unique perspective on the supply side of school choice. Whom does Edison aim to attract to its schools? Why? How does Edison find itself competing with public school systems through independent charters, yet assisting public school systems through district charters and district schools of choice? More generally, how does a supplier of public schools think about the market? What are the costs and benefits of serving different types of students? Do the incentives for supplying new schools of choice favor families who have traditionally had little to choose from or families who already enjoy quality schools and ample choice? Without revealing trade secrets, Edison's experience suggests that supply-side incentives favor the traditionally disadvantaged. School choice may not promote student selectivity or creaming. School choice may in fact help equalize educational opportunity.

Who Attends Edison Schools?

Edison Schools offers its public education partners—charter boards and traditional school boards—an education model that is designed to help all students, regardless of academic or socioeconomic background, succeed at high levels. The model

---

[10]Edison Schools Inc, *Fourth Annual Report on School Performance* (New York: Edison Schools Inc, October 2001).

is explicitly researched based. It attempts to bring together in a single comprehensive school design those wide-ranging factors shown consistently to influence student achievement and school performance. The factors include not only the obvious education variables—curriculum, instruction, and assessment—but also more general factors such as organization, leadership, management, technology, culture, and community.[11]

For example, the model provides for a nontraditional school organization based on academies, houses, and teams—devices meant to foster a strong sense of community and commitment, even in the largest schools. The curriculum in all Edison schools is organized around academic standards developed by Edison that meet or exceed the standards in every state. Instruction employs researched-based programs and practices, including *Success for All* for elementary reading, a K–12 math program developed through the *University of Chicago School Mathematics Project,* and science programs developed by one of the nation's premier organizations of science educators, *BSCS.*

Edison schools make extensive use of computers: all teachers are provided laptops, all students above second grade are provided computers for use at home, schools are equipped with classroom and lab computers, and all computers are networked locally and nationally, connecting Edison teachers, students, and families coast to coast. The schools also emphasize the arts, with every student taking a fine arts or music class daily. Notwithstanding the breadth of the program, the schools are decidedly focused—on academic achievement. Edison high schools, for example, offer only an academic track—and an extensive remediation program so that all students prospectively can be successful in an academic track.

The model is not aimed at a particular clientele. It includes elements that are targeted at students at risk of academic failure, such as *Success for All.* And it includes elements that are

---

[11]Extensive details on Edison's education program and school design are available on Edison's Web site <www.edisonschools.com>.

more characteristic of traditionally high-achieving schools, such as the math and science programs, the technology focus, and the academics-only high school. It is a model that would be well suited to poor and traditionally unsuccessful inner-city students or affluent and generally high-achieving suburban students.[12]

It may come as some surprise then to see who actually attends Edison schools. The vast majority of Edison's students are economically disadvantaged. Specifically, the average Edison school (see Table 1) has 70 percent of its students eligible for the federal government's free or reduced-price lunch program, an indicator of economic disadvantage in schools. Nor are these students a random slice of America's disadvantaged. Edison's students are primarily and disproportionately (that is, relative to America's poor generally) children of color. African Americans constitute 64 percent of the students at the average Edison school; Hispanics constitute 17 percent. On average, Caucasian enrollment at Edison's schools is only 16 percent, far below what it would be if Edison served all economically disadvantaged racial groups equally.[13]

TABLE 1

Demographics of Edison Schools, 2000–2001

School Demographic	Average School Percentage
African American	64%
Caucasian	16%
Hispanic	17%
Free/reduced lunch	70%
Number of schools	87

[12]On the history of the development of Edison's education program and school design, see John E. Chubb, "Lessons in School Reform from the Edison Project," in Diane Ravitch and Joseph Viteritti, *New Schools for a New Century* (New Haven, Conn.: Yale University Press, 1997).

[13]Nationwide the racial/ethnic distribution of families below the poverty line—a proxy for eligibility for free/reduced-price lunch—is 35 percent Caucasian, 32 percent African American, 28 percent Hispanic, and 5 percent Other. See U.S. Bureau of the Census, Washington, D.C., 2000.

Edison's students reflect in part the kinds of communities in which Edison schools have taken hold. Edison schools have a substantial presence in U.S. cities. Table 2 highlights the locations of all Edison schools open for the 2000–2001 school year, the last year for which complete demographic data are available (and when Edison operated 113 schools).[14] Although Edison offers schools in a wide range of communities, cities predominate. From big cities such as Boston, Washington, D.C., Baltimore, Atlanta, Miami, Detroit, Chicago, Minneapolis, Kansas City, Dallas, San Antonio, Denver, and San Francisco, to smaller cities such as Albany, Rochester, York, Macon, Flint, Wichita, Tyler, and Fresno, Edison schools are much more likely than not to be urban. The 2001–2002 school year saw this tendency continue, with new Edison schools opening in the cities of Las Vegas and Buffalo.

Cities, of course, are made up of a range of people, not only the disadvantaged. Location alone cannot explain why Edison schools are so heavily attended by poor and minority children. Even in cities, Edison schools could easily fill up with students from more advantaged backgrounds.[15] Edison schools are schools of choice. Although concerns about student selectivity would seem to predict a relatively advantaged enrollment, that has not happened. What accounts for Edison's student profile? It is not the schools' education program, which is well suited to high achievers. Could it be that some of the premises of the selectivity concern are wrong? Or are other factors at work to mitigate the forces of selectivity?

---

[14]Table 2 consolidates elementary, middle, and high schools that occupy a single building into one entry; hence the total number of schools in the table is somewhat less than 113.

[15]For example, urban private schools fill up rather easily with students from middle and upper class families looking for something either different (e.g., religious) or better (e.g., safer or more academically successful) than what the local public schools are offering. Many such families would seem potential candidates for (free) Edison schools. On private school choice, see: J. R. Betts and R. W. Fairlie, "Explaining Ethnic, Racial, and Immigrant Differences in Private School Attendance, *Journal of Urban Economics* 50 (2001): 26–51; and R. J. Buddin and J. J. Cordes, "School Choice in California: Who Chooses Private Schools," *Journal of Urban Economics* 44 (1998): 110–34.

TABLE 2
Edison Schools by State and Community, 2000–2001

School Name	City	State	School Name	City	State
Edison Brentwood Academy	East Palo Alto	Calif.	Flint Northwestern Community High School Edison Partnership	Flint	Mich.
Edison Charter Academy	San Francisco	Calif.	Garfield-Edison Partnership School	Flint	Mich.
Edison McNair Academy	East Palo Alto	Calif.	Inkster High School	Inkster	Mich.
Edison-Bethune Charter Academy	Fresno	Calif.	Meek-Milton Primary Academy	Inkster	Mich.
Feaster-Edison Charter School	Chula Vista	Calif.	Mid Michigan Public School Academy	Lansing	Mich.
Phillips-Edison Partnership School	Napa	Calif.	Mount Clemens Junior & Senior Academy	Mt. Clemens	Mich.
San Jose–Edison Adacemy	West Covina	Calif.	Southwestern Edison Jr. Academy	Battle Creek	Mich.
Starr King–Edison Academy	Long Beach	Calif.	Washington-Edison Partnership School	Battle Creek	Mich.
Academy-Edison Elementary School	Colorado Springs	Colo.	Williams-Edison Partnership School	Flint	Mich.
Emerson-Edison Partnership School	Colorado Springs	Colo.	Wilson-Edison Partnership School	Battle Creek	Mich.
Roosevelt-Edison Charter School	Colorado Springs	Colo.	YMCA Service Learning Academy	Detroit	Mich.
Timberview-Edison Junior Academy	Colorado Springs	Colo.	Edison/PPL School	Minneapolis	Minn.
Wyatt-Edison Charter School	Denver	Colo.	Kenwood-Edison Charter School	Duluth	Minn.
Wintergreen Interdistrict Magnet School	Hamden	Conn.	Raleigh-Edison Academy	Duluth	Minn.
Friendship Edison Public Charter School–Blow Pierce Campus	Washington	D.C.	Washburn Junior Academy	Duluth	Minn.
Friendship Edison Public Charter School–Carter G. Woodson Campus	Washington	D.C.	Allen-Edison Village School	Kansas City	Mo.
Friendship Edison Public Charter School–Chamberlain Campus	Washington	D.C.	Westport Edison Middle Academy	Kansas City	Mo.
Friendship Edison Public Charter School–Woodridge Campus	Washington	D.C.	Westport Edison Senior Academy	Kansas City	Mo.
Thomas A. Edison Charter School	Wilmington	Del.	Woodland-Edison Classical Academy	Kansas City	Mo.
Henry S. Reeves Elementary School	Miami	Fla.	Carver Heights–Edison Elementary School	Goldsboro	N.C.
Charles R. Drew Charter School	Atlanta	Ga.	Dillard-Edison Junior Academy	Goldsboro	N.C.

School	City	State
Martin Luther King, Jr.-Edison	Whitakers	N.C.
Riley-Edison	Trenton	N.J.
Jefferson-Edison Elementary School	Trenton	N.J.
Chicago International Charter School–Longwood Campus	Chicago	Ill.
Feitshans-Edison	Springfield	Ill.
Franklin-Edison School	Peoria	Ill.
Loucks Edison Junior Academy	Peoria	Ill.
Northmoor-Edison School	Peoria	Ill.
Dodge-Edison Elementary School	Wichita	Kans.
Edison-Ingalls Partnership School	Wichita	Kans.
Edison-Isley Partnership School	Wichita	Kans.
Jardine-Edison Junior Academy	Wichita	Kans.
Boston Renaissance Charter School	Boston	Mass.
Seven Hills Charter School	Worchester	Mass.
Gilmor Elementary	Baltimore	Md.
Furman Templeton Elementary	Baltimore	Md.
Montebello Elementary	Baltimore	Md.
Baylor Woodson Elementary School	Inkster	Mich.
Blanchett Middle School	Inkster	Mich.
Detroit Academy of Arts and Sciences	Detroit	Mich.
Detroit-Edison Public School Academy	Detroit	Mich.
Dr. Martin Luther King Jr. Academy	Mt. Clemens	Mich.
Edison-Oakland Public School Academy	Ferndale	Mich.
Edison-Perdue Academy	Pontiac	Mich.

School	City	State
Swift Creek-Edison Elementary	Macon	Ga.
Granville Charter High School	Macon	Ga.
Granville Charter Middle School	Davenport	Iowa
Granville Charter School	Trenton	N.J.
Schomburg Charter School	Jersey City	N.J.
New Covenant Charter School	Albany	N.Y.
The Charter School of Science & Technology	Rochester	N.Y.
Dayton View Academy	Dayton	Ohio
The Dayton Academy	Dayton	Ohio
Lincoln-Edison Charter School	York	Pa.
The Renaissance Academy–Edison Charter School	Phoenixville	Pa.
Edison-Blair Academy	Dallas	Tex.
Edison-Henderson Academy	Dallas	Tex.
Edison-Hernandez Academy	Dallas	Tex.
Edison-Maple Lawn Academy	Dallas	Tex.
Edison-Medrano Academy	Dallas	Tex.
Edison-Runyon Academy	Dallas	Tex.
Edison-Titche Academy	Dallas	Tex.
Elm Creek Elementary School	Atascosa	Tex.
Kriewald Road Elementary School	San Antonio	Tex.
McNair-Edison Junior Academy	San Antonio	Tex.
Scobee-Edison Junior Academy	San Antonio	Tex.
Stewart-Edison Junior Academy	Tyler	Tex.
Milwaukee Academy of Science	Milwaukee	Wisc.

GOVERNANCE AND SELECTIVITY

All Edison schools operate under one of three basic governance structures. "District contract" schools are organized by the policies of local public school systems and are accountable by contract to the local board of education (or in one case, Baltimore, to a state board of education that has taken control of low-performing district schools). District contract schools can take many forms: existing schools or new ones, closed schools slated for reopening, failing schools or schools aiming to offer an alternative program. Whatever the case, a school district contracts with Edison to implement its school design and be accountable for all school operations and performance. "District charter" schools are organized by the charter school policies of a state but are accountable to a local school board, and sometimes a community charter board as well. District charters can come into being because an existing district school elects, by teacher and parent vote, to "secede" from district governance and operate as a charter, or because a group interested in starting a charter school successfully petitions the local school board to authorize a new charter school. Finally, "independent charter" schools are organized under the charter school policies of a state and are accountable either directly to a state or to a state-authorized chartering authority such as a public university. Independent charter schools operate completely outside of local district policies and control.[16]

However Edison schools are organized and governed, they are enrolled as schools of choice. Independent charter schools are enrolled entirely on the basis of choice: they have no assigned students; enrollment is strictly voluntary. Every student who attends an independent charter is there because a parent or guardian has taken affirmative steps to enroll the student. In contrast, students come to district charter schools and district contract schools by a

---

[16]Each type of governance also represents a theoretically different way for contracting between the public and private (or independent nonprofit) sectors to improve education. On contracting, see Paul T. Hill, Lawrence C. Pierce, and James W. Guthrie, *Reinventing Public Education: How Contracting Can Transform America's Schools* (Chicago: University of Chicago Press, 1997).

range of means. Although several of Edison's district schools are filled by choice alone, most are filled by some form of "neighborhood preference" choice: students in a school's attendance zone have the first claim to seats in a school, after which students throughout the district can fill unclaimed seats by choice. These rules, though more restrictive than full choice, tend to bring a significant measure of choice to Edison's district schools.

Edison also asks that no student be compelled to attend an Edison school. Students are therefore free to opt out of their neighborhood school (implicit choice) if they or their families do not want Edison's program. Moreover, many of the schools that districts ask Edison to manage are low performing and therefore underenrolled. They have ample room for explicit choice students. Although district schools are generally not shaped by school choice to the same degree as independent charter schools are, all Edison schools are shaped by school choice.

So, how do enrollments in Edison schools differ with school governance? Well, not as concerns about selectivity might suggest. Independent charter schools, enrolled strictly through choice, are not on average more advantaged educationally than district schools are (Table 3). On the one hand, district Edison schools have levels of economic disadvantage (as reflected in lunch programs) that are somewhat higher on average than Edison independent charter schools: 76 percent in district contracts and 60 percent in district charters (a weighted average of 68 percent) versus 65 percent in independent charters. On the other hand, independent charter schools are much more likely to attract African American students (83 percent on average) than are district charter schools (36 percent) or district contract schools (62 percent). If selectivity works, as it is most feared to work, independent charters would not enroll such high percentages of students whose backgrounds predict academic difficulty.[17]

---

[17]The average level of economic disadvantage in Edison's independent charter schools (65%) is much higher than the rate in all charter schools nationally (39%) and in all public schools nationally (37%). The percentage of minority students in Edison's independent charter schools (90%) is also much higher than the percentage (52%) in charter schools nationally. U.S. Department of Education, *The State of Charter Schools 2000.*

TABLE 3
Demographics of Edison Schools by Type of
Governance, 2000–2001

School Demographic	Average School Percentage		
	Independent Charter	*District Charter*	*District Contract*
African American	83%	36%	62%
Caucasian	8%	31%	15%
Hispanic	7%	26%	20%
Free/reduced lunch	65%	60%	76%
Number of schools	26	16	45

Of course, these differences should not be overinterpreted. They certainly suggest that choice may not be leaving needy students behind. But the levels of disadvantaged or minority enrollment need to be viewed relative to the levels in their respective home districts. Perhaps independent charter schools are located in communities where African American and economically disadvantaged populations are unusually high; if so, these schools might be relatively more advantaged than they appear. Or district schools might be in areas with fewer disadvantaged or minority students; these schools might be more disadvantaged than they appear. Finally, demographics only begin to tell the story about students. Perhaps choice attracts high percentages of disadvantaged and minority families—but the families of the highest-achieving disadvantaged and minority students. If so, schools of choice could still be creaming.

HOME DISTRICTS

What, then, do we know about the communities in which Edison works? First, they are on average *less* disadvantaged than the families that Edison serves. Table 4 compares the demographics of Edison schools with the demographics of the public school systems in which Edison schools are located. On average, schools in the home districts of Edison

TABLE 4

Demographics of Edison Schools Compared
with Home Districts, 2000–2001

| | Average School Percentage | |
School Demographic	Edison Schools	Home District
African American	64%	42%
Caucasian	16%	34%
Hispanic	17%	19%
Free/reduced lunch	70%	61%

Note: Free/reduced lunch data exclude 11 schools and 4 districts where district data were unavailable.

schools have fewer students eligible for free or reduced-price lunch—61 percent versus 70 percent. Schools in the home districts of Edison schools have far fewer African American students—42 percent versus 64 percent—and far more Caucasian students—34 percent versus 16 percent. Only the percentages of Hispanic students are similar when Edison schools and schools in their home districts are compared, 17 percent and 19 percent, respectively. These data suggest that not only are Edison schools serving students who traditionally have had substantial educational needs, but also Edison tends to serve relatively more of these students than does the average public school in the communities in which Edison works. Again, this is not an outcome that concerns about student selectivity would predict.

But, how much does this outcome have to do with school choice? In Table 5 the demographics of Edison schools are compared with the demographics of their home districts, for each form of school governance in which Edison schools are involved. The picture is generally consistent with the one that has been emerging: school choice has not enabled Edison schools to cream the strongest students in their respective communities. Regardless of the form of governance, hence of school choice, Edison schools attract higher percentages than other local public schools of those students whose achievement

TABLE 5

Demographics of Edison Schools Compared with Home
District by Type of Governance, 2000–2001

| | Average School Percentage | | | | | |
| | Independent Charter | | District Charter | | District Contract | |
School Demographic	Schools	District	Schools	District	Schools	District
African American	83%	58%	36%	18%	62%	45%
Caucasian	8%	25%	31%	49%	15%	32%
Hispanic	7%	14%	26%	24%	20%	21%
Free/reduced lunch	65%	62%	60%	51%	76%	64%

has traditionally lagged behind national norms. Focusing just on the demographic categories that have lagged most consistently—economically disadvantaged students and African American students—Edison schools enroll higher percentages of these students than do schools in their respective home districts, under every form of governance.

The data do suggest that there may be forces at work on Edison's enrollment besides school choice. The percentages of economically disadvantaged students in Edison schools exceed the percentages in their home districts by wider margins in district contract and district charter schools than in independent charter schools—76 percent versus 64 percent, and 60 percent versus 51 percent, in contrast to 65 percent versus 62 percent. This contrast may reflect a preference of local school districts to locate Edison schools in high-poverty areas or a preference by Edison Schools Inc to access the revenue available for serving economically disadvantaged students and therefore to locate in needier areas. But ultimately families must choose or accept what Edison is offering.

The evidence in Table 5 suggests that families who traditionally have had significant educational needs are likely to choose change. Where Edison offers independent charters—and choice reigns free—African American families are much more likely than other families in the local school district to choose an Edison school: 83 percent of the students in Edison independent charter schools are African American compared with 58 percent in the local public schools. And again, the choosers, apart from ethnicity, are not the economically advantaged. The average percentage of students eligible for free or reduced-price lunch in an Edison independent charter school is 65 percent, compared with 62 percent in the local public schools.

These average tendencies are all the more impressive because they reflect consistent patterns across most Edison schools. Table 6 compares minority enrollment in each Edison school with minority enrollment in the home district of each Edison school. Specifically, Table 6 asks which has the higher percentage of the home district's largest minority group, the Edison school or the average district school? For example, if the largest minority group in a district is Hispanic, and the average district school is 50 percent Hispanic, the Edison school would need to have 51 percent Hispanic to qualify as enrolling a higher percentage of the largest minority group.

In 90 percent of all Edison schools—78 out of 87 schools where data were available for the district as well as for the Edison school—the Edison school enrolls a higher percentage of the largest local minority group than the average

TABLE 6

Edison Schools with Larger Percentage of Dominant Minority Group Than Home District, by Type of Governance, 2000–2001

Type of Governance	Number	Percentage
Independent charter	24/26	92%
District charter	14/16	88%
District contract	40/45	89%
All	78/87	90%

public school does. This high level of consistency is main-
tained for all types of governance: 92 percent for independent charters, 88 percent for district charters, and 89 percent
for district contracts. Edison schools, in community after
community, attract a higher percentage than the local public
schools do of the families often thought least likely to
choose.

Similar results obtain for economic disadvantage. Table 7
compares the percentage of students eligible for free or
reduced-price lunch in each Edison school to the average
percentage eligible in the home district of each Edison
school. In 52 out of 75 cases where data were available for
the district as well as for the Edison school, Edison schools
enroll a higher percentage of students from low-income
families than schools in their home districts do on average.
This tendency depends somewhat on governance. For independent charters, 54 percent of the Edison schools enroll
more economically disadvantaged students than the average
local public school enrolls. For district charters the percentage is 71 percent and for district contracts the percentage is
78 percent. The pattern of results here sharpens a difference
that emerged above. Although Edison schools are clearly
popular with economically disadvantaged families regardless
of how they are enrolled, and there is no evidence that Edison schools attract a more advantaged clientele than the local
public schools even when the schools are independent charters filled by choice alone, there is a tendency for Edison

TABLE 7

Edison Schools with Larger Percentage of Students Eligible for Free/
Reduced Lunch Than Home District, by Type of Governance, 2000–2001

Type of Governance	Number	Percentage
Independent charter	13/24	54%
District charter	10/14	71%
District contract	29/37	78%
All	52/75	69%

schools enrolled with district guidance to be more disadvantaged relative to local public schools than independent charters are. Edison schools do not cream, but choice is not the only source of their economic makeup.

BASELINE TEST SCORES

In the vast majority of communities in which Edison works, Edison schools attract disproportionate numbers of economically disadvantaged students and students of color. This tendency is true of Edison's independent charter schools (particularly with respect to students of color), where parents have complete freedom to choose schools, and it is true of Edison's district charter and contract schools, where choice is constrained. The choice of Edison schools has generally not depleted the local public schools of their more affluent or Caucasian students, nor concentrated those students in Edison schools. Choice, in Edison's universe, has not exacerbated inequalities. To the contrary, choice has offered all families the opportunity to pursue a different education for their children, and although a range of families have chosen Edison schools, poor and minority families have been more likely than other families to make that choice.

There is, however, one caveat before we conclude that selectivity may not be cause for inordinate concern. Race, ethnicity, and income have traditionally been associated with student achievement—or a lack thereof.[18] But a school that is relatively high in free or reduced-price lunch students or in African American students, as Edison schools are, may still be creaming. Schools of choice may attract the best students from communities that are largely poor and minority.

---

[18]See esp.: Christopher Jencks and Meredith Phillips, *The Black-White Test Score Gap* (Washington, D.C.: Brookings Institution Press, 1998); Christopher Jencks et al., *Inequality* (New York: Basic Books, 1972); and James Coleman et al., *Equality of Educational Opportunity* (Washington, D.C.: U.S. Government Printing Office, 1966).

This problem is explored first in Table 8. The baseline test scores of Edison schools are compared with the average test scores of all schools in the home district of the Edison school. The comparison involves all standardized tests mandated by states or local school districts. It focuses on tests taken either the year prior to Edison or during Edison's first year.[19] The purpose of the comparison is to determine the relative achievement of the students that Edison initially enrolls. Are they more or less accomplished than the students in the district as a whole? Who chooses? We know their race or ethnicity and their economic circumstances. But are they perhaps the strongest students from groups that traditionally have not achieved at high levels?

The table provides separate comparisons for schools taking criterion-referenced tests and schools taking norm-referenced tests. The table reveals that Edison begins work, on average, with schools where student achievement is much lower than district norms. Overall, the difference

TABLE 8

Baseline Test Scores of Edison Schools Compared with Home District, by Type of Governance, 1995–2000

Type of Governance	Criterion-Referenced Tests		Norm-Referenced Tests	
	Edison	Home District	Edison	Home District
Independent charter	25%	42%	26	42
District charter	34%	42%	28	37
District contract	38%	48%	33	55
All	34%	46%	32	45

---

[19]Baseline test scores employ scores from the school's first year with Edison if the school is new or is enrolling many new students. Baseline scores employ scores from the year prior to Edison if the school's enrollment with Edison is generally unchanged from the prior year. For details, see Edison Schools Inc, *Fourth Annual Report*.

is 12 points on criterion-referenced tests—an average school-wide passing rate of 34 percent in Edison schools versus 46 percent in local district schools. On norm-referenced tests the difference is 13 percentiles—Edison schools begin on average at the 32nd national percentile rank while the home districts of Edison schools average the 45th national percentile for the year their respective Edison schools open. The differences are meaningful for students, amounting to perhaps a grade level of difference in achievement.[20]

The differences between Edison and non-Edison students hold up regardless of governing arrangements. Indeed, the differences are greater for independent charter schools than for district charter and district contract schools. This is the reverse of the finding for economic disadvantage, and it is quite contrary to what concerns about selectivity would lead us to expect. Where parents have the complete freedom to choose—in independent charter schools—low-achieving students are especially likely, relative to local achievement levels, to choose an Edison school. The difference in norm-referenced test scores in Edison's baseline year between Edison's independent charter schools and local public schools is 17 points on criterion-referenced tests and 16 points on norm-referenced tests. This suggests that Edison attracts not only students from racial, ethnic, and economic groups that have not traditionally succeeded, but also students who are *actually not succeeding* on average. Edison schools do not cream the best students from the communities in which they work. Edison schools begin on average with students who are achieving below the norms of their local communities.

This conclusion is cemented with a look at the initial conditions of Edison schools on a school-by-school basis. Table 9 shows rather dramatically that a full 90 percent of

---

[20]For the relationship between national percentile ranks and grade equivalent scores, see, e.g., *Stanford Achievement Test, Ninth Edition, Technical Manual* (New York: Harcourt Brace, 1998).

TABLE 9

Edison Schools with Lower Baseline Test Scores Than Home District,
by Type of Governance, 2000–2001

Type of Governance	Number	Percentage
Independent charter	20/20	100%
District charter	13/16	81%
District contract	36/41	88%
All	69/77	90%

Edison schools open with students who are achieving below the average of their respective communities. Edison is not attracting the most successful students in the communities in which it works. This conclusion holds regardless of governing arrangement. Importantly, it holds where families have complete freedom of choice. In 100 percent of Edison's independent charter schools, the initial achievement level is lower than the achievement level in the home district.

Families that have exercised school choice through Edison are disproportionately families whose children are not succeeding academically. This is the bottom line, regardless of race, ethnicity, or economic disadvantage. It is also true that the families who have exercised school choice through Edison are disproportionately African American and poor. These are groups whose children have traditionally fared less well than the national average—and the families school choice is supposed to work against, if selectivity is a serious problem. And it matters very little whether choice is completely free, as it is in the lotteries of independent charter schools, or constrained by neighborhood preferences, as it is in district schools. There is some evidence that economic need may be a bit higher in schools if a district is involved, but there is also evidence that educational need may be higher in schools if only choice is at work. Overall, the pattern could not be clearer: the processes of school choice in which Edison schools have been involved since 1995 have produced schools that consistently and dis-

proportionately serve students with serious educational, social, and economic needs—students that concerns about selectivity suggest would not be well served. The question, of
course, is why?

Demand-Side Considerations

Part of the answer lies with the families who have chosen—
or have not chosen—Edison schools. These families, including tens of thousands who have enrolled their children in
Edison schools and many more who have not, represent the
demand for alternative schooling. Without direct evidence,
perhaps formal surveys of choosers and non-choosers, it is
impossible to say with confidence why families have or have
not selected Edison schools. Edison Schools Inc does not use
survey research to evaluate prospective markets for its
schools.[21] Edison does survey parents once they are enrolled
in Edison schools. Each spring an independent survey research firm polls the parents and guardians of every student
in every Edison school.[22] These surveys are designed to help
schools improve "customer satisfaction," and therefore
probe deeply what families like and dislike about their particular Edison school. But the surveys do not ask why families chose an Edison school, and, of course, they are not
administered to families who did not enroll in Edison
schools. To understand the mix of families Edison has attracted, and failed to attract, we must therefore engage in a
bit of speculation.

---

[21]Before Edison opened its first schools in 1995, the company did conduct extensive market research, but that was for the purpose of evaluating the demand
for the concept in the first place and market-testing elements of the education
program and school design. For details on the market research, see Chubb,
"Lessons in School Reform from the Edison Project."

[22]The surveys have been done annually since 1995 by Harris Interactive (formerly Gordon S. Black) of Rochester, N.Y. The survey also includes teachers and
students and provides an analysis, called *CSImpact*, of the factors most responsible
for each school's overall levels of satisfaction. Schools use the surveys and analysis
to improve their practices and increase parent, teacher, and student satisfaction.

The strongest finding, amid many strong findings, in the analysis of Edison's enrollment is the low levels of Edison's baseline test scores. Edison schools have attracted disproportionate numbers of families whose children are achieving below national, state, and community norms. This is probably the most telling finding of the entire analysis, more telling by far than the racial and economic findings that are consistent with it. The test scores suggest, pretty plainly, that the families most likely to choose Edison schools are those who believe their current schools are *failing their children educationally;* the choosers are not families whose children are doing satisfactorily but want something better. The choosers are also disproportionately poor and minority— groups we know from survey research are relatively dissatisfied with their public schools.[23] Although a range of families choose Edison schools, and the mix of families in typical Edison schools is broadly reflective of their respective communities, Edison's population skews toward the dissatisfied.

Selectivity concerns would lead us to believe that the families who have not fared well in existing schools would lose out in the process of choosing schools. Yet the evidence suggests that families who are relatively well served by existing schools are simply not the ones opting to change schools. We can only speculate why, but several reasons come immediately to mind. One is *risk*. Moving to a brand-new school without a track record in the community entails risk. Will the new school really do a better job than the current school? A family whose children are clearly succeeding may be reluctant to accept this risk and move, even if the new school looks very promising. A family whose children are performing only tolerably well, and therefore is dissatisfied, may also be reluctant to switch: there is a risk that the new school could be even worse. But a family whose children are just not succeeding—by local, state, or national norms—may be willing to accept the risk.

---

[23]Moe, *Schools, Vouchers, and the American Public.*

A related reason may be what economists would call *transaction costs*. Changing schools is potentially disruptive to children and their families. Friends may have to be left behind. School clubs and after-school activities will probably need to change. Commuting may become more burdensome, for children as well as their parents. Just as the risk that a new school may not prove better than the old school may scare off all but the most dissatisfied families, so too may the costs of making a change be too high except for those with little to lose.

Finally, there is the matter of what families see in what Edison offers. Edison knows that families like most the fact that Edison is offering a richer education than many families are accustomed to receiving. A longer school day and year, art or music every day, a foreign language beginning in kindergarten, a computer for use at home: these basic elements of Edison's education program appeal to families across the economic and racial spectrum.[24] But which families are going to see these elements as most attractive? In all likelihood, families whose schools are most lacking in them, which often means families in inner-city schools.

Concerns about student selectivity may be based on inadequate, or careless, assumptions about the decision process families are likely to go through in evaluating whether to make a change. The prevailing thinking is that parents who care most about education and are most adept at obtaining information about their options will prevail in a world of school choice. Undoubtedly this is true, all things being equal. But all things are never equal. Choice also involves risk, transaction costs, and ultimately some benefit from making a change. These factors will add up differently for different families. Choice involves giving up what one has for the promise of getting something better in return.

---

[24]Chubb, "Lessons in School Reform from the Edison Project."

The evidence from Edison schools suggests that families do not want to "mess with success," no matter how modest that success might be. The parents most likely to switch are not the parents who are always on the make for something better for their high-flying kids. The parents most likely to switch are those for whom the relative benefits of Edison schools are dramatic and for whom the costs of continuing academic failure outweigh the risks and costs of change. Particularly in these early years of charter schools and contract schools, choice may simply make the most sense to those families and students with the most to gain and the least to lose by making a choice.

A SUPPLY-SIDE PERSPECTIVE

Edison's education program and school design were developed to serve the full spectrum of students and schools served by public education. That was the company's express mission when it was launched in 1991 as the Edison Project, and it remains the company's mission today: to provide a "world-class education to all students."[25] Edison aims to offer a good educational choice for families and communities whether they are high-achieving or low-achieving, rich or poor. In fact, Edison serves a range of communities. For example, Academy Edison Elementary School in Colorado Springs is located in an upper-middle-class suburb near the U.S. Air Force Academy and serves a population where less than 10 percent of the students are eligible for free or reduced-price lunch. Edison schools serve predominately middle-class communities in San Antonio, Duluth, and Peoria, among other locations.[26] Every Edison school does not begin in academic difficulty.

Yet Edison has watched the demographic profile of its schools change systematically each year since it opened for

---

[25]For mission statement and supporting detail see Edison's Web site <www.edisonschools.com>.

[26]Edison also has schools serving low-income populations in these communities.

business. From the 1998–99 school year to the 2000–2001 school year the level of economic disadvantage in the average Edison school rose from 57 percent to 65 percent to 70 percent eligible for free or reduced-price lunch, and the proportion of African American students in the average Edison school rose from 46 percent to 55 percent to 64 percent.[27] Edison is prepared to serve students of all types, but increasingly it is serving students with the greatest needs.

Of course, Edison is not a monopoly provider. It must take demand such as it is. And the demand for Edison schools, as just outlined, leans toward the needy end of the economic and educational spectrum. But how does this demand intersect with Edison's interests as a supplier—with Edison's economic, as opposed to educational, interests? The answer is, positively.

First, Edison must maintain its schools at a high level of enrollment if it is going to receive the revenue it needs to cover its costs and earn a profit. Every Edison school is funded on a per pupil basis. The funding is set by state charter school law and/or by negotiations with local school boards and charter school boards. The funding level is roughly the average per pupil funding in the school district in which the Edison school is located. Edison must pay all the costs of the school from these funds, including the salaries of teachers and other school staff, books, and other instructional materials, technology, utilities—everything that goes into operating a school.[28] Because most of these costs are fixed, it is important to Edison financially that its schools are fully enrolled. Net revenue is maximized when a school is fully enrolled.

Because Edison obviously is loath to open a school in a location where enrollment will be a problem, enrollment prospects

---

[27]Edison Schools Inc, *Fourth Annual Report on School Performance.*

[28]Edison also must pay rent or mortgage expenses in its charter schools. Capital items such as books or technology are amortized. Certain services, such as transportation, may be provided by school districts and deducted from the per pupil fee.

become an important consideration during the development of
a contract for a new school. Edison wants to minimize the risks
that its schools will not be full. It does so through two strategies, the first of which is most important: Edison, in effect,
shares the risk with a partner. All Edison schools are partner-
ship schools—that is, they are schools organized jointly with a
school district or community group interested in providing an
educational alternative where there is already an identified
need. The need may be one experienced by a community group
that now wants to create its own charter school. Or the need
may be one identified by a school board or superintendent
looking at the schools for which they are already responsible.
Either way, if a school has the community support or political
support to be launched, it generally has a solid base for initial
enrollment.

Edison's partners thus far have been community groups
such as Friendship House in Washington, D.C., and Project
for Pride in Living in Minneapolis that work with the economically disadvantaged, or urban school systems that serve
disproportionately poor and minority families. Edison generally works with its partners to determine whether the support exists to launch and fill an Edison school before the
decision to write a contract is ever taken.[29] Experience indicates with a high degree of consistency that the partners and
communities most interested in creating new schools are
those that have been experiencing educational disappoint-
ment or failure. Experience also indicates that schools that
are targeted, through sponsorship or location, at families
who have generally not enjoyed successful schools fill most
rapidly.

This experience is reinforced after schools are opened for
enrollment, initial sign-ups are complete, and empty seats

---

[29]A dramatic exception to this practice occurred in New York City in
2000–2001, when the Board of Education designated five public schools for con-
version to Edison schools without consultation with the school communities.
The backlash from the schools scuttled the completion of the contract.

must still be filled. Edison does no national advertising, and obviously aims to keep its enrollment costs as low as possible. Edison therefore employs a second method to fill its schools—a range of relatively low-cost techniques to advertise and attract families, including radio ads, direct mail, parent nights at the school, auto dial calls (to hundreds of families, with a recording from the school principal), free transportation to visit the school, "door hangers" to get the word directly to every home, booths at community events, school festivals, barbecues, ice cream socials, giveaways or trinkets for kids, and free immunizations and health screenings. A few of these techniques—free transportation or free immunizations and health screenings—may appeal especially to the economically disadvantaged. But most of them are familiar retail strategies or tried-and-true school recruitment strategies that could be used whether the families targeted were rich, poor, or in between.

The point, then, is not that Edison has targeted particular families with its advertising and outreach. It is that the families who respond to these straightforward and relatively low-cost efforts tend disproportionately to be economically disadvantaged or educationally dissatisfied, or both. Edison has kept its schools enrolled at over 98 percent of their capacity, and at relatively little cost. It has done so by working with partners who have identified genuine educational needs in their communities and by accessing families who do not require much encouragement to recognize their educational needs. If Edison were aiming to fill its schools with families who were already satisfied, the effort would be considerably more expensive.

A second supply-side consideration is funding. Edison offers essentially the same educational program and school design whether it is serving a population that is disadvantaged or middle class. There are differences, of course. The school serving disadvantaged students will likely require more reading tutors, more small-group instruction, more social services, and perhaps more special education. These represent additional operating costs. The school serving disadvantaged students may also have more teacher turnover because teaching in such schools can be more challenging. This means more training and support costs. These differential costs are not trivial. They could easily add $200,000, or sometimes more, to the cost of a typical disadvantaged school.

But schools serving disadvantaged students or students with special needs are often, though not always, eligible for additional funding beyond a local per pupil average.[30] Economically disadvantaged students qualify a school for federal Title I funding. These funds can come to $500 per student or more, and easily exceed $200,000 per school. Many states offer their own "compensatory" or "at risk" funding, which depends on a school's economically disadvantaged population. Special Education students bring additional funding, as do English Language Learners, that is, students requiring bilingual education or English as a Second Language (ESL). None of these extra funds are large or, in the view of many educators, adequate to get the job done. However, the adequacy of the funds depends to a large degree on the nature of a school's core education program and how well that program serves the needs of all students.

Edison's education program and school design were conceived from the ground up to meet the needs of *all* students. The needs of many of the students for whom extra funding is available are met through schoolwide efforts, not through (expensive) extra programs, which almost inevitably deny students some of the regular instructional program. Edison still employs many specialists, such as special education and ESL teachers, but these teachers are working with students within a regular education program that is also meeting their needs. No money is saved in these specialized areas, but the results are likely to be better for the money spent. Overall,

---

[30]Some state charter school laws fold all state categorical funds into the calculation of a per pupil funding level for charter schools. In these states funding does not change with the composition of the school's student body.

schools serving economically disadvantaged students can make financial sense. The extra funds are sufficient to meet their needs if the effort is made, as Edison has done, to do so through the entire education program.

A third supply-side consideration is economies of scale. Edison must supervise and support the schools for which it is responsible. Edison is accountable to its clients for student achievement, customer satisfaction, and implementing the Edison school design, among other things. Edison is also accountable to its public shareholders for financial performance. Edison has therefore developed systems to train, inform, support, supervise, reward, and control its schools. Some of these systems are automated and centralized, but others are face-to-face activities and decentralized. When Edison schools are clustered geographically, Edison enjoys economies of scale at the system level. A single trainer or supervisor can cover more schools at less cost, using automobiles instead of airplanes, taking minutes for travel instead of hours.

It so happens that it is easier to achieve economies of scale serving disadvantaged students than serving others. Disadvantaged students are concentrated in the densely populated cores of urban areas. These students are also served by school systems that tend to include large numbers of schools. Each of the fifty largest school systems in the United States includes over one hundred schools.[31] School systems are Edison's most common clients. Edison has the potential to negotiate deals to operate multiple schools in a large system. In a small school system, Edison could not operate more than a single school if parents are to be given a choice. Therefore, because of economies of scale, Edison prefers contracts, such as it has in Dallas and Las Vegas, to operate six or more schools in a single urban area. Disadvantaged students, heavily represented in such locations, benefit from Edison's economic self-interest.

---

[31]National Center for Education Statistics, U.S. Department of Education, *Digest of Education Statistics 2000*.

A fourth supply-side consideration is the economic margin of the school itself. Because Edison's program and design are constant, the economics of local school systems tend to shape the economic viability of any Edison school. Edison schools generally adopt local salary levels, and then supplement them for the 200-day school year that Edison normally runs. Edison schools also generally adopt local class size norms.[32] Taken together, these two factors—teacher salaries and class sizes—determine most of a school's budget. Because Edison follows local custom, its core school budgets are essentially determined by the practices of local school systems. For an Edison school to yield an economic margin—to pay for Edison's support costs or overhead and to contribute to the company's profit—local school systems must themselves have "margins" or revenues that are not spent directly on teachers and classrooms.

Of course, school systems do have support or overhead costs of their own. The interesting fact is that these costs tend to be proportionately greatest in large urban school systems.[33] Although school finances vary considerably from state to state, as a general rule, Edison stands the best chance of operating schools with acceptable economic margins if the schools are part of large urban systems, or are charter schools located within large urban systems. This economic incentive likewise favors economically disadvantaged students.

---

[32]Edison does this for many reasons. First, even small reductions in class size are expensive (a one-student reduction in a typical 24-classroom school costs $168,000—in a school receiving a typical $7,000 per student) and provide no reliable education benefits. Large reductions in class size are simply not feasible with locally determined revenues. Second, increases in class sizes are bad for business—and often bad for instruction—because they discourage enrollment among families who, very commonly, see smaller classes as a sign of better schools.

[33]In large urban school systems the proportion of the budget spent on teacher salaries is 52 percent and the proportion spent on administration and support is 15 percent. The remainder goes for transportation, food service, utilities, and other operating costs. See John E. Chubb, "The System," in Terry M. Moe, ed., *A Primer on America's Schools* (Stanford: Hoover Institution Press, 2001), 39–40.

A fifth supply-side consideration is the distribution of funding within local school systems. Because public schools are typically not funded on a per-pupil basis, there is a tendency for schools serving the most disadvantaged students to, in effect, receive fewer dollars per student than schools in the same district serving less-disadvantaged students. This disparity occurs principally through the ability of teachers using seniority rules to transfer schools, a process that tends to concentrate veteran high-salaried teachers in economically better parts of town and beginning low-salaried teachers in worse parts of town.[34] When Edison is given the opportunity to run a school in a poor part of town, and is paid the average per-pupil revenue in the district to do so, the deal will often bring greater financial resources to the school than it has received in the past. This reallocation of funds benefits the economically disadvantaged students who choose to attend.

Finally, there is a supply-side consideration that would seem to have little to do with economics. This sixth consideration is politics—and it has a major impact on Edison's economics. Where in public education can suppliers like Edison do business most efficiently? Ultimately, the answer depends a great deal on politics. Politics can change, of course. But for the last decade the dominant movement in education politics has been *accountability*: setting standards, giving tests, and rewarding or punishing schools for their performance. The accountability movement has proved to be one that political conservatives and liberals can find reasons to unite behind.[35] Every state but one now has explicit academic standards, and most states back up their standards with tests and sanctions. These systems vary enormously in quality and consequence, but one consistent effect of them

---

[34]See Hill, in this volume.

[35]Among the many fine works on this subject, see: Diane Ravitch, *National Standards in American Education* (Washington, D.C.: Brookings Institution Press, 1995), and The Koret Task Force, *Accountability* (Stanford: Hoover Institution Press, 2002).

has been to focus public attention on schools that are clearly failing. In state after state, schools can find themselves placed on "low-performing lists," and threatened with various penalties including closure and state takeover.

The accountability movement has been good for Edison. Superintendents under pressure to get schools off of low-performing lists are interested in using Edison to spur academic turnarounds. States faced with the prospect of taking over local schools are coming to Edison looking for a partner. Edison's business was spurred in 2000 by both of these developments. Dallas Independent School District contracted with Edison in 2000 to manage seven schools, including three of twelve on its low-performing list that year. The Maryland State Board of Education contracted with Edison to manage three schools it had taken over from the Baltimore City Schools for low performance. The state of Pennsylvania in 2001 contracted with Edison to run ten of eleven schools in Chester-Upland, a highly disadvantaged school system on the state's "empowerment" list. In August 2001, Governor Tom Ridge of Pennsylvania hired Edison to formulate a plan for improving the academic and financial performance of the entire Philadelphia public school system, also on the state's empowerment list. The accountability movement has heightened government interest in Edison, and prospectively other firms like Edison. In the process, the movement has made it better business for providers of education to focus on the needs of the disadvantaged.

LOOKING AHEAD

As policymakers consider the use of school choice to improve the quality of education, they would do well to look at the hard data on how school choice has actually worked in the United States in recent years. There is much that is not known about the costs and benefits of school choice. And there are good theoretical reasons to be hopeful as well as concerned. Until recently, one could only infer how choice might work as a broad strategy of school reform. Private schools, schools of choice in other countries, urban magnet schools, and other imperfect approximations of a system of school choice have been used by scholars and partisans for a generation to debate the merits of this systemic reform. Reliance on weak imitations should begin to come to an end.

With the advent of charter schools, contracting, and even widespread experiments with vouchers, hard evidence on systems much closer to the systemic reforms being proposed for the United States is becoming available. Arguments that heretofore could only be settled indirectly with evidence can now be confronted head on. Perhaps the most important of these arguments is that over student selectivity. Does school choice lead to creaming—to increased inequity and segregation? This is a vital question, all the more so because public education aspires to provide equal opportunity to all Americans.

The experience of Edison Schools is a large and instructive one. In nearly one hundred schools of choice the traditionally disadvantaged—the poor, children of color, low achievers—did not fail to choose. They found their way to Edison schools in larger numbers than did their more advantaged peers. This occurred, moreover, whether the schools were filled entirely on the basis of choice or through choice constrained by district policy. And on close inspection, it turns out there are good reasons why this may be so. The demand for alternatives may favor the interests of the most disadvantaged, at least in the short term until the risks of changing schools are reduced. The supply of alternatives may also be tilted toward the disadvantaged. Edison serves those families and communities who want to be served; it is also good business to do so.

5

Will Quality of Peers Doom Those Left in the Public Schools?

Eric A. Hanushek

Much is uncertain about the total effects of a broad voucher program on education. The United States has relatively limited experience with choice in general and vouchers in particular, and that experience has occurred in rather narrowly prescribed experiments. It is therefore difficult to project the results of a broader voucher program by simply expanding on past experience with such a program. On the other hand, considerable experience relates to various aspects of schools that have been highlighted as potentially important. This chapter concentrates on one such area—the role of school peers—and describes what related research has to say about this potential avenue of voucher effects.

THE CONTEXT FOR DISCUSSION

Of the many arguments that are made about the impacts of public schools, the one that generally lingers is "Vouchers will ruin the public schools." This argument frequently refers mainly to fiscal effects: vouchers would send funds that previously went to public schools to private schools. If funding were not increased, the overall budget for the public schools would decline, leading to the commonly hypothesized adverse fiscal impacts on existing public schools.[1] These arguments go beyond the scope of this chapter, but they are not the only aspects of potential impact on the public schools. A central concern revolves around how changes in the composition of students affects the students remaining in the public schools. The pejorative version of this concern is that the public schools would become the "dumping ground" for unmotivated and unprepared students; that is, that any good students would necessarily opt out of the public schools, leaving just the poorest students.

The important dimension of this issue is how other students in a school affect each individual's ability to learn. If there were no important interactions among students that affected individual learning, the fact that the public schools took on a population more difficult to educate would not necessarily be a damning statement. Since there will always be unmotivated and unprepared students, and they must be served someplace, the public school system is a natural place.[2] But to the extent that peers directly influence the quality of education, further attention is needed.

There are many dimensions of peer effects that deserve consideration. The most obvious one—the possibility of

---

[1]Of course, the number of students would decline with the fiscal support. Therefore, the real issue is whether any decline in funding is more or less than the costs of educating the departing students. The funding of any vouchers and its impact on public schools depends on the precise characteristics of any voucher, but the general issue is whether the marginal cost of the students departing schools is greater than the lost revenue. Any lost revenues, it should be noted, would be determined not only by the funding formula but also by political economy forces that determine overall support for public schools.

[2]Part of this discussion really considers issues that are simply a distraction. If, for example, all the best students left the public schools for private schools, the average achievement in the private schools would necessarily exceed that in the public schools. But this would have nothing to say about the value-added of either public or private schools; that is, it would not indicate which schools were contributing the most to student learning. As is well known, the movement of students from one school to another can affect the absolute and relative levels of average achievement in each, depending on where in the distribution moving students start and end up. All this can happen without changes in achievement of any individual student.

intensified racial concentration—has received significant attention. Indeed, the long history of racial separation in schools has been a subject of policy attention and concern since well before the 1954 U.S. Supreme Court decision in *Brown v. Board of Education.* The half-century of judicial and policy interventions aimed at eliminating disparities in racial composition and in other related characteristics of schools have their underpinnings in presumptions about the impacts of peers on student outcomes.[3]

But the racial dimension of peers is not the only dimension of potential importance. Although race has special impact because of history and legal status, similar peer concerns have been raised about the possibilities of divisions according to the socioeconomic status of students and their families. The current system, largely based on neighborhood attendance boundaries for schools, leads to substantial separation of students along the lines of income. Historically, segregation by income has been less pervasive than that by race, although it has been substantial. Further, recent attention has focused on the potential adverse effects of high concentrations of poverty.

The influence of student peers can naturally extend beyond these areas of attention. Although not usually linked to voluntary choices and vouchers, the potential impact of achievement and ability of peers offers another avenue of effects. Much of this discussion has previously centered on ability grouping in classrooms, but it could be relevant in a system of choice if schools tended to separate according to achievement levels.

Vouchers and choice also have potential interactions with special education. Considerable attention has been focused on special education because of its growing importance and expense. The Individuals with Disabilities Education Act, or IDEA, translated concerns about the education of children with both physical and mental disabilities into federal law

---

[3]See, e.g., David J. Armor, *Forced Justice: School Desegregation and the Law* (New York: Oxford University Press, 1995).

with its enactment in 1975.[4] This Act prescribed a series of diagnostics, counseling activities, and services for disabled students. From its inception when some 8 percent of public school students were placed in special education, the program has grown to 13 percent of the public school population. Identified students were given legal rights to an education appropriate for them.[5] The general thrust has been to provide regular classroom instruction where possible ("mainstreaming") along with specialized instruction to deal with specific needs. This aspect of school policy and law enters the discussions here for two reasons. First, one concern about voucher schools and other competitive schools is that they will generally exclude special needs students, thereby increasing the concentrations of special education in the public schools.[6] Second, if special education students are generally placed in regular classrooms, they could potentially disrupt the learning activities and adversely affect the regular education students.

The prior discussion of peer effects highlights how classmates directly affect the learning environment. Through their interactions in the classroom and school, students can alter the pace and character of learning. Yet there are still

---

[4]This Act, P.L. 94–142, was originally the Education for All Handicapped Children Act and was retitled IDEA in 1990. It is commonly identified as having direct and significant effects on the cost and methods of delivery of local education. See the discussions and evaluations in: William T. Hartman, "Policy Effects of Special Education Funding Formulas," *Journal of Education Finance* 6 (fall 1980): 135–59; Judith D. Singer and John A. Butler, "The Education for All Handicapped Children Act: Schools as Agents of Social Reform," *Harvard Educational Review* 57, no. 2 (1987): 125–52; David H. Monk, *Educational Finance: An Economic Approach* (New York: McGraw-Hill, 1990); Hamilton Lankford and James Wyckoff, "Where Has All the Money Gone? An Analysis of School District Spending in New York," *Educational Evaluation and Policy Analysis* 17, no. 2 (1995): 195–218.

[5]See Singer and Butler.

[6]The primary manifestation of this concern has been fiscal, with the public schools worried that their expenses will rise without adequate revenues flowing in. The best estimates of the cost of service provision place it at 2.3 times that for regular education; see Stephen Chalkind, Louis C. Danielson, and Marcus Brauen, "What Do We Know About the Costs of Special Education? A Selected Review," *Journal of Special Education* 26, no. 4 (1993): 344–70.

other avenues that might lead to attributes of peers affecting public school outcomes. Most important, teachers and schools might react to the composition of the student body in their own decisions. Of course, this could go either way, because officials may devote energy and resources in a compensatory manner or in a manner that reinforces student background deficits. The relevant dimensions here include both the actions of administrators and the private actions of teachers in their choices of schools.

One final aspect of voucher influences on peer composition deserves attention. A lot depends on how the expanded voucher program affects the equilibrium patterns of school choice and movements, but the overall impact on the amount of school mobility can itself be relevant for learning. Specifically, if there is more or less movement between schools, the stability of the learning process could be affected.

The goal of this chapter is to sort through what is known about these various aspects of peers. The focus is entirely on what evidence exists about interactions between various aspects of peers and student outcomes. In particular, the discussion does not consider whether increased choice would alter each aspect of peers. Instead, it asks the simple question, "If the identified aspects of peers do change, what impact should we expect?"

WHY THIS IS A DIFFICULT QUESTION

A central issue in the analysis of peer influences on student performance is the difficulty of such investigations. The typical structure of studies into peer effects would relate some measure of school outcomes to individually relevant factors and to characteristics of peers. From statistical analyses, the studies attempt to infer the impact of peers. The difficulty in this is making sure that the observed relationship really reflects the causal impact of peers—and not just other factors that tend to coincide with differences in peers. Three general and significant issues arise in such an analysis.

First, most studies of the effects of peers rely on data about student outcomes and peer groups that are naturally generated by schools. But our observations of schooling circumstances are the result of the choices of schools (and implicitly peers) that are made by individual families and, to some extent, by school administrators. Thinking initially of the choices of families, which most often result from choices of residential location, we can be quite certain that they are not random. These choices, although frequently motivated by a number of factors beyond schools such as incomes or job locations, will reflect the preferences and opportunities facing individual families. This simple fact—that there is a purposeful element in the individual choices of families—implies that some of the outcomes for student performance may result from characteristics of families that, although entering into their decisions, are not obvious or easily measured. For example, the parents most concerned about the schooling of their children may provide the best family environment for learning and also pay particular attention to their choice of school location. That being so, it can be difficult to sort out the separate influences on student performance and to identify the impact of peers per se, particularly when parents at a school tend to make similar choices.

Similarly, school administrators often make decisions about resources and classroom composition with some underlying purpose in mind. They may try to place their best teachers with students most in need or to group students according to an estimate of their entering abilities. These decisions can again confuse the effects of peers and the effects of school inputs—that is, misidentify the causal impact of peers on achievement as opposed to other family or school differences that are the real causes.

Second, the ability to distinguish the separate effects of individual and school factors from those of peers depends crucially on observing and measuring the significant inputs into student performance. The typical analysis, however, does not have perfect measures of either family background or school inputs. For example, from the perspective of family inputs into achievement, researchers typically have available only a few crude measures of background, often lacking even basic characteristics such as the education level of parents. The details of school quality and school inputs, too, may be known only imperfectly. On the other hand, the consistency of choice of schools across families implies that there is a strong tendency for parents who have similar backgrounds and aspirations to select a common school, and there is an additional likelihood that school quality will have a similar effect on not just the individual student but on the student's peers. As a result, measures of peer backgrounds and performance may provide reasonably accurate surrogates for the individual's characteristics (which are measured with error). In other words, the characteristics of others in the classroom and school may act as a partial measure of the individual's characteristics. The importance of this is that imperfect measurement will push common statistical analyses toward overstating the impacts of peers. Even when peers have no true impact, for example, they may appear significant just because the peer measurements effectively provide additional information about the individual student.

Finally, one must sort out causal influences. It is not sufficient to know that, say, peer characteristics are associated with individual characteristics and performance. One needs to know whether this association results from peer attributes and interactions causing the observed differences in student performance. The reason for this is also straightforward: if one is to ascertain the impacts of peers, and of possible alterations in the composition of peers, the analysis must capture the amount of difference that the peers cause as opposed simply to selecting peers with certain characteristics or to residing together because of common decision-making processes. This issue of causation pervades most analyses of student performance but is most acute when analyzing peers.[7] The inherent tendency for peers with similar attributes and motivations to cluster together makes associations of performance across peers very likely and builds in difficulties in inferring the causal aspects of the various associations.[8]

These issues are introduced to underscore the uncertainty that surrounds much of the discussion of peer influences. Although a variety of statistical and analytical techniques have been employed to sort out the various factors, they prove to be difficult to deal with completely. The discussion below will note where the uncertainty is particularly large. But one significant implication is that much of the prior work fails to provide much of a sound basis for understanding the impacts of peers on achievement.

INDIVIDUAL PEER INTERACTIONS

The discussion in this section concentrates on how characteristics of peers—characteristics that might change with expanded choice—affect the classroom and student learning. Subsequent discussions broaden the topic to include other ways in which peers can influence results.

---

[7]For example, it is common to employ income measures to proxy differences in family background that might be important for student learning or other outcomes, but there are serious questions about whether the relevant causal factor is income per se or some other attributes that are related to income; see Susan E. Mayer, *What Money Can't Buy: Family Income and Children's Life Chances* (Cambridge, Mass.: Harvard University Press, 1997).

[8]An additional problem, which we do not dwell upon here, is the reciprocal relationship between the individual student and peers. The underlying idea behind peer influences is that the others in a classroom and school affect the character of learning. But if that is true, then it is natural to believe that the individual student also affects all his or her classmates—implying that the direction of causation for any observed association is unclear. This problem, crucial in some kinds of analyses, is difficult to deal with in many studies. This issue, sometimes referred to as the "reflection problem," is described technically in Charles F. Manski, "Identification of Endogenous Social Effects: The Reflection Problem," *Review of Economic Studies* 60 (July 1993): 531–42; and Robert A. Moffitt, "Policy Interventions, Low-level Equilibria, and Social Interactions," in S. Durlauf and H. P. Young, eds., *Social Dynamics* (Cambridge, Mass.: MIT Press, 2001).

RACE/ETHNICITY

As mentioned, the first issue generally raised about added choice is the worry that the amount of racial isolation may increase and that this will adversely affect performance, particularly by black students left behind. Is there evidence that peer racial composition affects achievement for blacks as well as for Hispanics and other minorities? The decision in *Brown v. Board of Education* asserted this to be the case, ruling that separate but equal was unconstitutional in the case of education because separate could not be equal.

In addition to legal controversy about the underlying research leading to the Supreme Court decision, considerable immediate attention was given to understanding the educational implications of school segregation and desegregation.[9] Much of the analysis was conducted during the early periods of school desegregation. The analyses of effects of desegregation have considered a wide variety of outcomes, ranging from measures of racial interactions to achievement. This discussion concentrates on achievement aspects, although some attention is given below to other aspects.

The landmark legislatively mandated civil rights report on the *Equality of Educational Opportunity* and its offshoot provide empirical evidence that racial isolation harms academic achievement.[10] Subsequent work by Crain and Mahard; Boozer, Krueger, and Wolkon; and Grogger also find that school racial composition affected academic, social, and

---

[9]The Supreme Court decision included one reference to the evidence on harmful results of segregation. The famous footnote 11 documented the findings of doll studies by Kenneth and Mamie Clark that showed low self-esteem of black children in the segregated South; see Kenneth Clark and Mamie Clark, "The Development of Consciousness of Self and the Emergence of Racial Identity in Negro Children," *Journal of Social Psychology* 10 (1939): 591–99.

[10]See James S. Coleman et al., *Equality of Educational Opportunity* (Washington, D.C.: U.S. Government Printing Office, 1966), and U.S. Commission on Civil Rights, *Racial Isolation in the Public Schools* (Washington, D.C.: U.S. Government Printing Office, 1967).

economic outcomes.[11] In contrast, Cook and Evans conclude that the available evidence found that desegregation has little if any effect on mathematics and reading achievement in elementary school, and Rivkin finds no evidence that exposure to whites increased academic attainment or earnings for black men or women in the high school class of 1982.[12] Overall, there remains considerable disagreement about the nature and magnitude of benefits of desegregation efforts, let alone about their costs.[13]

The contrasting findings and lack of consensus concerning the importance of school racial composition emanate in large part from the difficulty of isolating the causal impact of peer characteristics. For example, if families with greater resources or a greater commitment to schooling tend to choose schools with lower concentrations of minorities, the racial composition effects are easily confounded with other factors.[14] In the studies of school racial composition effects, for example, neither Crain and Mahard (1978) nor Boozer, Krueger, and Wolkon (1992) provide many statistical controls for differences in socioeconomic background or prior

---

[11]See: Robert L. Crain and Rita E. Mahard, "Desegregation and Black Achievement: A Review of the Research," *Law and Contemporary Problems* 42, no. 3 (1978): 17–53; Michael A. Boozer, Alan B. Krueger, and Shari Wolkon, "Race and School Quality Since *Brown v. Board of Education,*" *Brookings Papers: Microeconomics*, 1972, pp. 269–338; Jeffrey T. Grogger, "Does School Quality Explain the Recent Black/White Wage Trend?" *Journal of Labor Economics* 14, no. 2 (1996): 231–53.

[12]See: Michael D. Cook and William N. Evans, "Families or Schools? Explaining the Convergence in White and Black Academic Performance," *Journal of Labor Economics* 18, no. 4 (2000): 729–54; Steven G. Rivkin, "School Desegregation, Academic Attainment, and Earnings," *Journal of Human Resources* 35, no. 2 (2000); 333–46.

[13]See, e.g., the reviews in Robert Crain, "School Integration and Occupational Achievement of Negroes," *American Journal of Sociology* 75, no. 4, Part II (January 1970): 593–606; Armor, *Forced Justice*; Janet Ward Schofield, "Review of Research on School Desegregation's Impact on Elementary and Secondary School Students," in J. A. Banks and C. A. M. Banks, eds., *Handbook of Research on Multicultural Education* (New York: Macmillan, 1995).

[14]For a discussion of the link between family preferences and neighborhood location, see Charles M. Tiebout, "A Pure Theory of Local Expenditures," *Journal of Political Economy* 64 (October 1956): 416–24.

academic preparation, but still leave open questions about the adequacy of background measures. Grogger (1996) does use a longitudinal data set that contains information on family background and achievement measures, although it is unlikely that this small number of variables would account for all factors that are related to both outcomes and the choice of schools. The inclusion of private school students in the analysis further increases the likelihood that the school racial composition coefficients are biased upward. Rivkin (2000) uses school district aggregate measures of exposure to whites in order to overcome the nonrandomness of both neighborhood location within districts and attendance in non-neighborhood schools; nevertheless, unobserved differences among districts may contaminate the estimates.

In a recent paper, Hoxby uses differences in school racial composition for adjacent cohorts to identify the causal effect of peer group composition.[15] The estimates from this procedure imply that school racial composition is generally important for blacks. For example, they suggest that differences between blacks and whites in school racial composition can explain perhaps one-fifth of the elementary school black/white reading differential.

Another investigation of school racial composition by Hanushek, Kain, and Rivkin, although not completely independent, pursues a related methodology to isolate the effects of racial composition on the growth in achievement.[16] Their analysis considers patterns of the racial composition across grades and across different school years. They find that

---

[15] Caroline Minter Hoxby, "Peer Effects in the Classroom: Learning from Gender and Race Variation," Working paper no. 7867, National Bureau of Economic Research, August 2000. Hoxby's estimates pertain to scores at different grade levels. The largest effects appear in the third grade, with smaller effects of performance at later grades.

[16] Eric A. Hanushek, John F. Kain, and Steve G. Rivkin, "New Evidence About *Brown v. Board of Education*: The Complex Effects of School Racial Composition on Achievement," National Bureau of Economic Research, December 2001. Both Hoxby (2000) and this paper by Hanushek, Kain, and Rivkin use data from Texas schools, although the years and methodology for the analyses differ.

racial composition effects are centered on the performance of black students. The fact that racial composition does not have nearly as strong an effect on either white or Hispanic students indicates that it is not simply a result of different school resources. Moreover, the effects of racial composition are borne largely by high-ability black students who suffer most significantly from increased proportions of black students in their schools.

When these results are translated into potential national effects (as measured by the national gaps on the National Assessment of Educational Progress, or NAEP), it is estimated that past changes in racial composition of U.S. schools could account for a substantial portion—if not all—of the closing of the racial-achievement gap that occurred in the 1980s.[17]

The findings in areas other than achievement are more difficult to characterize, in part because the quality of the underlying research is quite mixed. In examining reviews of desegregation effects on nonachievement outcomes, Schofield concludes that "desegregation has no clear-cut consistent impact" on African American self-concept or self-esteem (p. 607), and that "the evidence taken as a whole suggests that desegregation has no clearly predictable impact on student intergroup attitudes" (p. 609).[18] Although each of these conclusions is heavily qualified, the research makes it clear that the currently available evidence does not indicate that these wider outcomes are places of systematic impact.[19]

---

[17]Eric A. Hanushek, "Black-White Achievement Differences and Governmental Interventions," *American Economic Review* 91, no. 2 (2001): 24–28. For a general discussion of changes in the black-white achievement gap and the potential causes of this narrowing, see Christopher Jencks and Meredith Phillips, eds., *The Black-White Test Score Gap* (Washington, D.C.: Brookings Institution Press, 1998).

[18]Schofield, "Review of Research on School Desegregation's Impact on Elementary and Secondary School Students" (1995).

[19]Note, however, that this summary of evidence concentrates mainly on specific desegregation effects and not just the racial composition of schools.

Socioeconomic Status (SES)

Much of the attention given to socioeconomic status has concentrated on issues of neighborhood poverty and, particularly, how concentrations of poverty affect individual outcomes. This discussion of neighborhood poverty emphasizes employment and crime outcomes, along with reference to schooling.[20] For example, Mayer finds that SES (and racial composition) of the school affects high school completion of both whites and blacks—but measures of characteristics of schools other than student body composition are missing.[21]

In a forthcoming study, Hanushek et al. find that the direct analysis of achievement effects of low-income peers does not indicate that poverty concentrations have a significant negative effect on student performance.[22] The income measure is, however, relatively imprecise.

---

[20]For discussions of a wide range of issues related to neighborhood poverty concentrations, see: Christopher Jencks and Paul E. Peterson, eds., *The Urban Underclass* (Washington, D.C.: Brookings Institution Press, 1991); Paul A. Jargowsky, *Poverty and Place: Ghettos, Barrios, and the American City* (New York: Russell Sage Foundation, 1997); and Katherine M. O'Regan and John M. Quigley, "Accessibility and Economic Opportunity," in C. Winston, J. A. Gomez-Ibanez, and W. Tye, eds., *Essays in Transportation Economics* (Washington, D.C.: Brookings Institution Press, 1999). For more recent investigations relying on randomization of people who leave bad neighborhoods, see: James E. Rosenbaum and Susan J. Popkin, "Employment and Earnings of Low-Income Blacks Who Move to Middle-Class Suburbs," in Jencks and Peterson, eds., *The Urban Underclass* (1991); James E. Rosenbaum, "Changing the Geography of Opportunity by Expanding Residential Choice: Lessons from the Gautreaux Program," *Housing Policy Debate* 6, no. 1 (1995): 231–69; Lawrence F. Katz, Jeffrey R. Kling, and Jeffrey B. Liebman, "Moving to Opportunity in Boston: Early Results of a Randomized Mobility Experiment," *Quarterly Journal of Economics* 116, no. 2 (2001): 607–54; and Jens Ludwig, Greg J. Duncan, and Paul Hirschfield, "Urban Poverty and Juvenile Crime: Evidence from a Randomized Housing-Mobility Experiment," *Quarterly Journal of Economics* 116, no. 2 (2001): 655–69.

[21]Susan E. Mayer, "How Much Does a High School's Racial and Socioeconomic Mix Affect Graduation and Teenage Fertility Rates?" in Jencks and Peterson, eds., *The Urban Underclass* (1991).

[22]Eric A. Hanushek, John F. Kain, Jacob M. Markman, and Steven G. Rivkin, "Does Peer Ability Affect Student Achievement?" *Journal of Applied Econometrics* (forthcoming).

Peer Ability

The analysis of peer ability and achievement has been particularly problematic from a statistical viewpoint.[23] Students in a common classroom have many shared educational experiences, so that the quality of questions or the amount of disruption affects all the students. From an analytical viewpoint, each student contributes to the classroom experience and is simultaneously affected by those same experiences. Moreover, common factors such as the impact of a particularly good teacher will heighten the common experiences and, if teacher quality is not well measured, lead to biases in understanding peer influences. These situations make it virtually impossible to separate out the effects of current classroom behavior on individual achievement. The import of this is largest when considering the influence of other students' ability and achievement on learning.

By distinguishing between the ability of peers and their current behavior, we can, however, gain some insights. Specifically, measuring peer ability by their prior achievement levels tends to break any direct relationship of current interactions, teacher quality, and the like, making possible some insights into how the level of achievement of other students influences individual performance.

Attempts to estimate peer effects on educational achievement in this way have been relatively limited. Hanushek (1972, 1992) finds no peer achievement effects when looking at achievement growth in individual classrooms.[24] On

---

[23]The chief problem has revolved around the simultaneous determination of achievements by all students in the classroom. Formal statements of the problem can be found in Manski, "Identification of Endogenous Social Effects" (1993); Moffitt, "Policy Interventions, Low-level Equilibria, and Social Interactions" (2001); and William A. Brock and Steven N. Durlauf, "Interactions-Based Models," in *Handbook of Econometrics* (forthcoming).

[24]See two studies by Eric A. Hanushek: *Education and Race: An Analysis of the Educational Production Process* (Cambridge, Mass.: Heath-Lexington, 1972), and "The Trade-off Between Child Quantity and Quality," *Journal of Political Economy* 100, no. 1 (1992): 84–117.

the other hand, Henderson, Mieszkowski, and Sauvageau (1976); Summers and Wolfe (1977); and Zimmer and Toma (2000) report positive influences of higher-achieving peers at least for some students; importantly, Summers and Wolfe find stronger effects of peers for low-income students.[25]

Consideration of ability tracking in schools likewise has yielded mixed results.[26] A common policy thread has been that low-achieving students benefit from being in classes with high-achieving students but that high-achieving students are unaffected by classroom composition. If this were the case, heterogeneous classroom groupings would seem the most desirable in that they would maximize performance of low achievers at no cost. However, this presumption has been challenged on the grounds that detracking or tracking is a zero-sum game in which losers balance winners.[27] Nonetheless, these studies have faced a number of the statistical problems, in part because measures of the school inputs have not been particularly reliable.

Our own attempt to investigate peer ability suggests that the level of achievement of others in the classroom has a small but significant influence on performance.[28] It also suggests that the effect is relatively constant across achievement levels. Thus, any movement toward more homogeneous schools and classrooms in terms of ability would imply both

---

[25]See: Vernon Henderson, Peter Mieszkowski, and Yvon Sauvageau, *Peer Group Effects and Educational Production Functions* (Ottawa: Economic Council of Canada, 1976); Anita Summers and Barbara Wolfe, "Do Schools Make a Difference?" *American Economic Review* 67, no. 4 (1977): 639–52; Ron W. Zimmer and Eugenia F. Tuma, "Peer Effects in Private and Public Schools Across Countries," *Journal of Policy Analysis and Management* 19, no. 1 (2000): 75–92.

[26]See, e.g.: Jeannie Oakes, "Can Tracking Research Inform Practice? Technical, Normative, and Political Considerations," *Educational Researcher* 21, no. 4 (1992): 12–21; Laura M. Argys, Daniel I. Rees, and Dominic J. Brewer, "Detracking America's Schools: Equity at Zero Cost?" *Journal of Policy Analysis and Management* 15, no. 4 (1996) : 623–45.

[27]See Argys, Rees, and Brewer.

[28]Hanushek, Kain, Markman, and Rivkin (forthcoming).

winners and losers—with the high-achieving students being the biggest winners and low-achieving students the losers.

Whether more homogeneous classrooms is appropriate policy of course remains a hotly debated issue. If the primary objective is raising the achievement of those on the bottom, ensuring more heterogeneous classrooms would further that objective. On the other hand, the higher-achieving students in the U.S. have not performed particularly well compared with higher-achieving students in other countries, implying that performance at the top should not be ignored.

Special Education

The final attribute of individual peers is the impact of special education. Although special education has occupied school policy considerations at all levels, including legislatures and courts, the discussions have virtually never involved any evidence about student outcomes. Nor have there been extensive investigations of the fiscal impacts, although the existing investigations suggest that current funding has left regular education worse off when there is a larger special education population.[29]

The one analysis of how special education affects the learning of regular education children does not suggest any adverse effect.[30] Moreover, although difficult to do with certainty, it does not appear that more extensive mainstreaming of special education students has a more detrimental effect.[31]

---

[29]See Hamilton Lankford and James Wyckoff, "Where Has the Money Gone?" (1995), and by the same authors, "The Allocation of Resources to Special Education and Regular Instruction," in H. F. Ladd, ed., *Holding Schools Accountable: Performance-based Reform in Education* (Washington, D.C.: Brookings Institution Press, 1996); also, Julie Berry Cullen, "Essays on Special Education Finance and Intergovernmental Relations," dissertation, Massachusetts Institute of Technology, 1997.

[30]Eric A. Hanushek, John F. Kain, and Steve G. Rivkin, "Inferring Program Effects for Specialized Populations: Does Special Education Raise Achievement for Students with Disabilities?" *Review of Economics and Statistics* (forthcoming).

[31]The uncertainty in this analysis is due to the lack of detailed information about the decision to place students in mainstreamed or other programs.

DECISIONS OF SCHOOLS AND TEACHERS

School personnel and programs are not simply set in the abstract without consideration of the students they will serve. On the contrary, the allocation of school resources is a very complicated process, involving politics, individual choices, legal rulings, and more. For example, current fiscal legislation in a variety of states determines the funding going to a district in part based on the income of the community (and implicitly of the students), and federal funding for compensatory programs (Title 1) goes to disadvantaged students. Some of these allocations are required or reinforced by court orders in a variety of state funding cases. Furthermore, individual families make choices of communities that undoubtedly reflect to some extent the characteristics of students. Once having chosen a community, they will also tend to participate in the determination of local funding and of local programs.

It is obvious that the changing choices of schools under a voucher program could realign some of the politics and funding decisions currently seen. For example, a shifting school population could make given districts eligible for different amounts of state and federal funding, but it could also alter the political support for a district's schools if more residents shifted to private schools.

The political outcomes that might result from a large-scale voucher program are entirely too speculative to enter into here. Although there are some hints about the effects of past decision-making related to the composition of schools, it is unclear how any of the evidence can be generalized to an altered organizational form for vouchers.[32]

---

[32]For example, the original analysis of the effects of racial composition in U.S. Commission on Civil Rights (1967) suggested that schools with more concentrated black populations had lower achievement. However, that analysis did not consider any school factors that might have affected achievement, and subsequent analysis suggested that racial composition had a small effect on student achievement (Hanushek 1972). One interpretation of these contrasting results is that resources were skewed against black students and that the political process reacted to the composition of schools. Nevertheless, without explicit analysis of the politics of resource allocation, it is possible to generalize to other stuations.

One area where existing evidence may, however, give insights involves the behavior of teachers. Over a long period of time it has been recognized that teachers tend to exercise choices in deciding where to teach and that these tend to be related to characteristics of the student body. In particular, several analyses suggest that teachers systematically search out schools with a more affluent population.[33] Extensions of this suggest that teachers also want higher-achieving students.[34] Further, white teachers (but not black teachers) appear to search out schools with a higher concentration of white students. This behavior of teachers could lead to alterations in the public school teaching force if vouchers alter the characteristics of the student body.

STUDENT MOBILITY

One final consideration relates to potential impacts on the level of student mobility from a move to vouchers. Little is known about how a voucher system would evolve, but it could change the character of the public schools, depending on the population that opted out for the voucher schools. For example, if the families that tended to take up the vouchers were also the more stable families—those that tended not to relocate their students—the average mobility rates of students in the public schools could rise. In other words, by removing part of the stable base population of a school, the remaining population tends to change schools more frequently.

The relevance of this is that schools with higher mobility rates tend to have a less coherent structure of instruction.

---

[33]See David Greenburg and John McCall, "Teacher Mobility and Allocation," *Journal of Human Resources* 9, no. 4 (1974): 480–502; and Richard J. Murnane, "Teacher Mobility Revisited," *ibid.*, 16, no. 1 (1981): 3–19.

[34]Erik A. Hanushek, John F. Kain, and Steve G. Rivkin, "Why Public Schools Lose Teachers," Working paper no. 8599, National Bureau of Ecomonic Research, November 2001.

A high mobility rate lessens the amount of learning, even for students who themselves do not move.[35] The effect may be relatively small for any year, but it becomes more important for students who stay in schools with high mobility rates over substantial portions of their school career.

CONCLUSIONS

Will the public schools left after the introduction of vouchers deteriorate in quality because of the loss of important "high value" peers? Answering this question requires projecting how the peer composition might change along with understanding the impacts of any changes in peers. This chapter concentrates entirely on the latter issue: the impact of peer composition on student achievement.

Inferring the potential impact of the introduction of a widespread voucher program is difficult because we have little relevant experience. Nonetheless, in a variety of instances, existing information can provide insights. To assess the potential impact we divide the analysis into a series of compositional measures of the classroom: racial composition, the socioeconomic status of peers, the ability level of classmates, and the special education status of other students. We also consider more aggregate impacts: changed resource allocations, variations in the supply of teachers, and increased rates of student mobility.

The available evidence suggests that the largest concern would come from changes in the racial composition of public schools. Specifically, black students would appear to be hurt if there were significant increases in the proportion of their classmates who also were black. The evidence further suggests that the effects of racial composition apply only to blacks and not to other minorities or to whites.

---

[35]Hanushek, Kain, and Rivkin, "Disruption Versus Tiebout Improvement: The Costs and Benefits of Switching Schools," Working paper no. 8479, NBER, September 2001.

On a related point, because teachers respond in their choice of schools to the student body composition—including race—significant changes in student body composition might call for efforts to ensure a supply of high-quality teachers. This concern, of course, applies with equal or greater force to current schools.

6

How School Choice Affects the Achievement of *Public* School Students

Caroline M. Hoxby

Opponents of school choice often take the view that schools can be "only so good," so that what some students gain, other students must lose. This view of schools becomes most obvious when issues like "cream skimming" are discussed. The usual argument runs as follows: If the better students leave the regular public schools to attend choice schools, the students who remain in regular schools will be worse off. In fact, evidence suggests that the choice schools created by recent reforms do *not* cream skim. Nevertheless, cream skimming is a theoretical possibility, and we should care about the outcomes of students who remain in regular public schools, especially in the short term, when regular public schools are likely to contain the bulk of students.

THE IMPORTANT EFFECTS OF SCHOOL CHOICE ON *PUBLIC* SCHOOL STUDENTS

Experts on school choice, particularly those with a background in economics, find the view that schools can be "only so good" to be strange. As a rule, *the* key way in which organizations respond to competition is by becoming more efficient. This tendency is so strong that we often say that an organization has "become more competitive" when what we really mean is that it has become more efficient or productive in response to competition. Thus, it is not only possible, but likely, that regular public schools will respond to competition from choice schools by raising their pupils' achievement or raising another pupil outcome valued by parents. Better outcomes are the way in which a regular public school would evince increased efficiency. This is because existing choice reforms are designed so that per pupil spending in the regular public schools cannot fall when a student leaves to attend a choice school. In fact, under all but one existing reform, a regular public school's per pupil spending actually *rises* when a student leaves.

In short, although achievement might fall in regular public schools if choice introduces cream skimming and only cream skimming, it might rise if regular public schools raise achievement in order to compete with choice schools. In this chapter, I examine how *public* school students' achievement was affected by three important, recent choice reforms: vouchers in Milwaukee, charter schools in Michigan, and charter schools in Arizona. I study these three reforms because they are the only ones in which the choice schools can, legally, garner a large enough share of enrollment to provide a nonnegligible amount of competition for the regular public schools. In fact, because even these choice reforms are still modest in size, I attempt to see whether public schools respond competitively when they face the loss of only 6 percent of their enrollment. Looking at early evidence, as I do, is the worst case for school choice. When a school has lost only a bit of its enrollment for only a few years, it might not respond competitively or respond in any way. Yet, the first few percent of students who leave could easily be the most attractive (extreme cream skimming). Thus, if I find evidence that public schools raise achievement when faced with early and minor competition from choice schools, the results are likely to understate the improvement in achievement that regular public schools would attain when faced with more sustained, more substantial competition.

Because evidence on recent choice reforms necessarily has a short-term character, I also review evidence on how traditional forms of choice in the United States affect the achievement of *public* school students. In particular, I examine the effects of parents' being able to choose among public school districts by choosing their residence. This is the dominant form of choice that exists in the United States currently, but the availability of multiple school districts differs a great deal from one metropolitan area to another. I also review results based on parents' being able to choose private schools in the metropolitan area easily because their local private schools charge subsidized tuition.

Because choice schools in Michigan and Arizona are charter schools (and therefore supervised by the states' departments of education), complete information on the students they enroll is available. Therefore, I directly examine the race, ethnicity, and poverty of charter school students in the two states, comparing them with the student populations from which the charter schools draw. I look directly, in other words, for evidence that the charter schools are enrolling students who are unusual, given the populations from which they draw.

COULD REGULAR PUBLIC SCHOOLS RAISE ACHIEVEMENT?

It is very plausible that competition could stimulate regular public schools to raise achievement enough to swamp any adverse effects that choice might have via cream skimming. Perhaps it is useful to take a brief step back from the issue of school choice and think about another formerly public industry that is less controversial but that illustrates the same concerns. In the parcel post industry, the United States Postal Service (USPS) had a monopoly. When lawmakers proposed to allow private firms (like United Parcel Services, Federal Express, and DHL) to compete with the USPS, some commentators issued dire warnings. The private firms, they argued, would cream skim the most profitable parcel post customers, and the common person's parcel service would deteriorate profoundly. They argued that USPS could not improve, and its parcel service would be slower, have fewer options, and so on if private firms were allowed to take some of its best customers. Exactly the opposite reaction has occurred. USPS is now far more efficient in parcel post than it was when it had a monopoly, and it has introduced new services, like Express and Priority parcel service, that make its customers better off. Customers who use the private firms' services are also better off, because they are getting better service than the USPS formerly gave them. With hindsight, the average person now sees that the USPS *was* able to improve when faced with competition and that the positive reaction to competition swamped other forces that might have led USPS parcel service to deteriorate.

In the school choice debate, there is obsessive interest in the question of "who wins" and "who loses" when choice is introduced. This obsession may turn out to be a mistaken application of energy. Choice need not make some students into losers and others into winners. It is at least possible that all students will be better off. Because students who remain in public schools are clearly the group whose "winning" is most in doubt, my focus in this chapter is exclusively on their achievement. (I should note here in passing that in a number of other studies that have examined the achievement of students who use vouchers or charter schools, the evidence suggests that students who enroll in choice schools have better achievement after one or more years. These "choice students," however, will not concern me further.)

I examine public school students in three states because only three choice reforms fulfilled some commonsense criteria. If we are interested in studying cream skimming and public schools' competitive reaction, it is necessary that the public schools actually faced nonnegligible competition. At a bare minimum, the choice program should be such that (1) there is a realistic possibility that at least 5 percent of students ordinarily enrolled in regular public schools could go to choice schools, (2) the regular public schools lose at least some money (not necessarily the entire per pupil cost) when a student goes to a choice school, and (3) the reform has been in place for a few years. The reforms that satisfy these basic requirements are school vouchers in Milwaukee, charter schools in Michigan, and charter schools in Arizona. I describe each of these reforms below. Apart from these three reforms, most choice reforms fail to meet at least one of these requirements. In particular, choice reforms are typically characterized by constraints on enrollment (for instance, no more than one percent of local students can attend choice schools) or perverse financial incentives (for instance, the local district loses no money when it loses a student to a choice school, so that its per pupil spending rises as it loses students).[1]

The Effect of Vouchers on Milwaukee Public School Students

Vouchers for poor students in Milwaukee were enacted in 1990 and were first used in the 1990–91 school year. Currently, a family is eligible for a voucher if its income is at or below 175 percent of the federal poverty level (at or below $17,463 for a family of four).[2] For the 1999–2000 school year, the voucher amount was $5,106 per student or the private school's cost per student, whichever was less. For every student who leaves the Milwaukee public schools with a voucher, the Milwaukee public schools lose state aid equal to half the voucher amount (up to $2,553 per voucher student in 1999–2000). Milwaukee's per pupil spending in 1999–2000

---

[1]For a thorough review of current school choice reforms, see Nina Shokraii Rees, *School Choice 2000: What's Happening in the States* (Washington, D.C.: Heritage Foundation, 2000). In most cases where I have not used materials directly obtained from the relevant state's department of education, I have relied upon Rees for a description of reforms.

[2]As a rule, any child who is eligible for free or reduced-price lunch is also eligible for a voucher. The actual cut-off for reduced-price lunch is 185 percent of the federal poverty level, but the difference between 175 percent (the cut-off for the vouchers) and 185 percent is not rigorously enforced (and would be difficult to enforce).

was $8,752 per pupil, so the district was losing 29 percent of
the per pupil revenue associated with a voucher student.
Currently, the vouchers may be used at secular and nonsecu-
lar private schools.[3]

The voucher program had a difficult start. Although approximately 67,000 students were initially eligible for
vouchers, participation was initially limited to only 1 percent
of Milwaukee enrollment (later, from 1993 to 1997, 1.5 percent). Also, the future of the program was in doubt for its
first eight years, owing to a prolonged court dispute over its
legality. The dispute was resolved in 1998, after which the
program not only became more certain but also became better funded and ten times larger, with a ceiling of 15 percent
of Milwaukee enrollment.[4] Overall, although the voucher
program that started in 1990 might have been expected to
have had a small impact on the Milwaukee Public Schools
beginning with the 1990–91 school year, the program generated very little potential competition until the 1998–99
school year. At the same time, because the program was already somewhat established and familiar to Milwaukee residents by 1998, one would expect a quicker response to this
program than to a completely new program. In short, it is
plausible to look for a productivity impact, if any, over the
few most recent school years. The 1996–97 school year effectively predates serious competition.

Not all schools in Milwaukee experienced the same increase
in competition as the result of the voucher program. The

---

[3]The information on the Milwaukee program and Wisconsin public schools is
obtained from several publications of the Wisconsin Department of Public Instruction: *Knowledge and Concepts Examinations: Test Results*, electronic file;
Milwaukee Parental School Choice Program: Facts and Figures; *Reading Com-
prehension Test Results*, electronic file; *School Finance Data*, electronic file; and
School Performance Report, electronic file—all Madison, 2000.

[4]The future of the program is still somewhat in doubt. First, opinions of the state
Supreme Court disagree on the question of whether it is constitutional to have vouchers that can be used at schools with religious affiliation; it is likely that the United States
Supreme Court will eventually rule on this matter. Second, the Wisconsin legislature
has threatened to fund the vouchers at such a low level that they would be unusable.

greater a school's share of poor children, the greater was the potential competition because the greater was the potential loss of students. Some Milwaukee schools had as few as 25 percent of their schools eligible for vouchers; others had as many as 96 percent eligible. Also, because private elementary schools cost significantly less than private high schools, more than 90 percent of vouchers were used by students in grades one through seven in 1999–2000. Thus, only elementary schools in Milwaukee faced significant potential competition.

These facts about the voucher program suggest that the following type of evaluation is most appropriate for examining the effect of vouchers on Milwaukee public school students. First, one should focus on achievement in grades one through seven. Second, achievement should be compared from 1996–97 (before significant competition) to 1999–2000 (after significant competition). Third, schools in Milwaukee can be separated into two groups. In schools that "faced more competition," a large share of students were eligible for vouchers, and cream skimming or competitive response should be more acute. In those that "faced less competition," a smaller share of students were eligible and the cream skimming or competitive response should be correspondingly smaller. In the language of medical experiments, the schools that faced more competition got the full treatment and the schools that faced less competition got a partial treatment. As in medical experiments, it is desirable to find some schools that were not treated at all: "control schools." I chose a control group of schools from Wisconsin that most closely matched Milwaukee's schools in urbanness, their shares of black and Hispanic students, and their poverty rates. Finding control schools was not easy because Milwaukee's schools are much poorer and have much larger shares of minority students than most other schools in Wisconsin. Because the control schools are slightly less disadvantaged than the Milwaukee schools, they initially had better achievement and higher achievement growth. In other words, if vouchers had no effect at all, the control schools would be expected to improve relative to Milwaukee schools, simply because more advantaged schools tend to improve relative to less advantaged ones.[5] Thus, the evidence I present is likely to *understate* slightly any improvements that took place in Milwaukee's schools.

Table 1 shows some demographic indicators for the three groups of elementary schools: 32 Milwaukee schools that faced more competition (those in which at least two-thirds of students were eligible for vouchers), 66 Milwaukee schools that faced less competition (those in which less than two-thirds of students were eligible for vouchers), and control schools that faced no competition.

In the schools that faced the most competition, an average of 81.3 percent of students were eligible for free or reduced-price lunch (hence eligible for vouchers), 65.4 percent of students were black, and 2.9 percent of students were Hispanic. In the schools that faced less competition, an average of 44.5 percent of students were eligible for vouchers, 49.1 percent of students were black, and 13.7 percent of students were Hispanic.[6]

I included a Wisconsin elementary school in the control group if it (1) was not in Milwaukee, (2) was urban, (3) had at least 25 percent of its students eligible for free or reduced-price lunch, and (4) had black students compose at least 15 percent. Only twelve schools in Wisconsin met these criteria. In the control schools, average enrollment in a grade was 51 students, 30.4 percent of students were eligible for free or

---

[5]It is fairly obvious that more advantaged schools will have better achievement if we do not control for demographic differences among students. It is less obvious that more advantaged schools will have better achievement *growth*, but they do in fact. For instance, prior to 1996, Wisconsin elementary students took statewide tests in reading (only). In the pre-voucher period, achievement growth was negative in Milwaukee schools, based on these tests. In contrast, achievement growth was positive in the schools that form the control group.

[6]Note that these demographic numbers reflect what the schools looked like in 1990, *before* the voucher program was enacted. This is the correct method for choosing treated and control schools. One does not want to measure the extent of treatment using measures of student composition that potentially reflect how students reacted to the voucher program.

TABLE 1

Pupil Characteristics in Schools That Were Faced with More Competition,
Less Competition, and No Competition from Vouchers in Wisconsin

	Percentage of Students Eligible for Free/Reduced-Price Lunch	Percentage of Students Who Are Black	Percentage of Students Who Are Hispanic
Schools faced with more competition	81.3	65.4	2.9
Schools faced with less competition	44.5	49.1	13.7
Schools faced with no competition (control schools)	30.4	30.3	3.0

Sources: Wisconsin Department of Public Instruction (various 2000) and United States Department of Education, *School District Data Book.*

Note: Schools faced with more competition are Milwaukee elementary schools where at least two-thirds are eligible for free or reduced-price lunch (hence also vouchers). There are 32 such elementary schools, each of which has an average fourth-grade enrollment of 72 students. Schools faced with less competition are Milwaukee elementary schools where fewer than two-thirds of students are eligible for free or reduced-price lunch (hence vouchers). In all these schools, at least 30% are in this category; 66 schools, each with an average fourth-grade enrollment of 71 students. Control schools are all the Wisconsin elementary schools that are urban, have at least 25% eligible for free lunch, and have at least 15% black students. Schools in this category: 12, each with an average fourth-grade enrollment of 51.

reduced-price lunch (and, therefore, would have been eligible for vouchers had they lived in Milwaukee), 30.3 percent of the students were black, and 3.0 percent of students were Hispanic.

Students in Wisconsin take statewide examinations in grades 4, 8, and 10. Because I am focusing on the reactions of elementary schools, I use the fourth-grade score, expressed in national percentile rank points (NPR), on five tests: mathematics, science, social studies, language, and reading. It is worth noting that during the period in question Wisconsin enacted a controversial reading curriculum that emphasized whole-language methods, as opposed to phonics.

Table 2 shows the results of comparing the three groups of schools before and after the voucher program created significant competition in 1998. Examine the top panel, which shows achievement on the math exam. In 1996–97, the schools that later faced the most competition attained 34.5 NPR points. In 1999–2000, they attained 53.3 NPR points, an annual gain of 6.3 points. The schools that ultimately faced less competition attained 33.7 NPR points in 1996–97 and 48.2 NPR points in 1999–2000, an annual gain of 4.8 points. Math achievement in the control schools grew from 50 NPR points in 1996–97 to 60.6 NPR points in 1999–2000, an annual gain of 3.5 points. Clearly, math achievement grew the most in the schools that faced the most competition from vouchers, less in the schools that faced less competition, and the least in the schools that faced no competition.

Without going through all of the numbers for science, social studies, language, and reading, we can look down the right-hand column of Table 2 and immediately see the same pattern for all subjects. In every subject, achievement grew most in the schools that faced the most voucher competition, a medium amount in the schools that faced less competition, and the least in the schools that faced no competition. The pattern holds even in reading and language, where the controversial curriculum may have been responsible for the lower rates of achievement growth, which are actually negative for schools that were not faced with a lot of competition from vouchers.

Overall, an evaluation of Milwaukee suggests that public schools made a strong push to improve achievement in the face of competition from vouchers. The schools that faced the most potential competition from vouchers raised achievement dramatically. Growth of four or more NPR points per year is highly unusual in education, yet Milwaukee schools managed such improvements in math, science, and social studies. Recall, moreover, that the achievement effects of vouchers are likely to be understated because the control schools contain slightly more advantaged students.

TABLE 2

Fourth-Grade Test Scores in Schools Faced with More Competition,
Less Competition, and No Competition from Vouchers in Wisconsin

	1996–97	1999–2000	Annual Change
Math NPR Score			
Schools faced with more competition	34.5	53.3	6.3
Schools faced with less competition	33.7	48.2	4.8
Schools faced with no competition (control schools)	50.0	60.6	3.5
Science NPR Score			
Schools faced with more competition	31.9	52.8	7.0
Schools faced with less competition	32.3	49.7	5.8
Schools faced with no competition (control schools)	56.0	62.9	2.3
Social Studies NPR Score			
Schools faced with more competition	41.6	54.2	4.2
Schools faced with less competition	43.4	50.7	2.4
Schools faced with no competition (control schools)	61.0	65.6	1.5
Language NPR Score			
Schools faced with more competition	41.8	49.4	2.5
Schools faced with less competition	41.8	46.2	1.5
Schools faced with no competition (control schools)	53.4	53.2	− 0.1

TABLE 2 *(continued)*

	1996–97	1999–2000	Annual Change
Reading NPR Score			
Schools faced with more competition	44.2	46.5	0.8
Schools faced with less competition	45.1	43.6	−0.5
Schools faced with no competition (control schools)	59.0	55.0	−1.3

Sources: Wisconsin Department of Public Instruction (2000 various) and United States Department of Education, *School District Data Book.*

Note: Test scores are measured in national percentile points. Statistics are based on weighted averages over schools in the relevant group, where each school is weighted by its enrollment.

The Effect of Charter Schools on Michigan Public School Students

In 1994, Michigan enacted a charter school law as part of a series of changes in its method of financing schools. Michigan charter schools receive a per pupil fee that is essentially the same as the state's foundation level of per pupil spending (the state's minimum level of per pupil spending, given the characteristics of the school's student population). For instance, in 1999–2000, the average charter school student in Michigan had $6,600 spent on his education, whereas the average regular public school student had about $7,440 spent on his education. Detroit public schools spent $8,325 per pupil and the average charter school student in Detroit had about $6,590 spent on his education. A district that loses a student to a charter school loses approximately the foundation level of per pupil revenue. Charter competition tends to be most substantial in the elementary grades because the charter fees more adequately cover costs for the lower grades. By the 1999–2000 school year, approximately 3.5 percent of all nonprivate elementary students in Michigan were enrolled in charter schools. The corresponding number for secondary students was 0.7 percent. Charter schools can receive their charters from statewide organizations, such as universities, so they can compete with local public schools, unlike charter schools in many other states that have their charters granted and renewed by their local district.[7]

I evaluate the effect of charter schools on Michigan public school students in much the same way as I evaluated the effect of the Milwaukee voucher program. I separate schools into those that faced charter competition and those that did not, and I compare their performance before and after charter competition. I focus on elementary grades because public elementary schools felt most of the charter competition. Michigan students take exams in the fourth, seventh, and tenth grades, so I show results for the fourth and seventh tests. Michigan tests its students in math and reading, and the tests are scored in scale points (like the familiar SAT-I test). A scale point is worth between 1.25 and 2.5 percentile points, depending on the test and grade.

A few issues arise with Michigan that did not arise with Milwaukee. In Wisconsin it was easy to define *ex ante* the treatment and control schools: Schools outside of Milwaukee faced no competition, and Milwaukee schools faced competition that depended simply on the share of their students who were poor enough to be eligible for vouchers. In Michigan, "treatment" and "control" and "before" and "after" must be defined on a district-by-district basis, where a district is being "treated" and is in the "after" period once it is forced to recognize that it is losing a critical share of students to charter schools. Of course, we do not know what this critical share might be, but it is useful to know that the mean year-to-year change in a Michigan school's enrollment *prior to 1994* was 5.1 percent. Therefore, a

---

[7]Information on Michigan charter schools and all the data on Michigan schools are taken from the following publications of the Michigan Department of Education, Lansing (all 2000): *Directory of Michigan Public School Academies*; *K–12 Database*, electronic file; *Michigan Educational Assessment Program and High School Test Results*, electronic file; and *School Code Master*, electronic file.

small drawing away of enrollment by a local charter school would be hard to differentiate from normal year-to-year variation in enrollment. However, a persistent drawing away of enrollment of more than 5 percent, say, would be likely to be noticed and attributed to charter schools. I initially looked for a critical level of 6 percent, and because it worked well, I kept it. A critical level of 7 or 8 percent works very similarly.[8] In short, I say that a Michigan school faces "charter competition" if at least 6 percent of the students enrolled in its district are enrolled in charter schools.[9]

The left-hand columns of Table 3 list the Michigan districts in which charter schools account for at least 6 percent of total enrollment inside the district's boundaries. There are 597 districts in Michigan and only 34 listed in the table, so a nonnegligible charter school presence is still the exception and not the rule. Districts of all sizes, including Michigan's large city districts, are represented among the districts that face charter school competition. Detroit, Lansing, and Kalamazoo all have at least 6 percent of enrollment in charter schools.

The Michigan districts that had to face competition from charter schools probably were not a random group of districts. Charter schools may have formed as a response to

---

[8]Results for a critical level of 7 or 8 percent are available from the author. If one chooses a critical level much higher than 8 percent, the results depend unduly on just a few districts—simply because only a few districts ever face more than an 8 percent drawing away of their students. Descriptive statistics for the Michigan data set are also available from the author.

[9]Note that the charter schools' share of local enrollment is based, in Table 3, on the assumption that students attend charter schools in the district in which they reside. Because students who are in particularly unappealing districts are disproportionately likely to attend a charter school outside their district if they do attend a charter school, the statistics on which the table is based slightly understate the enrollment losses of bad districts. It is possible to construct estimates of the share of a district's students who attend charter schools, but such estimates are somewhat noisy and (in any case) generate results that are qualitatively similar to the results shown in Table 4. The alternative set of results may be found in the working-paper version of this chapter, available from the author.

TABLE 3

Michigan School Districts and Arizona Municipalities
Where at Least 6% of Pupils Entered Charter Schools

Michigan School Districts		*Arizona Municipalities*	
Alba	Huron	Avondale[a]	Keams Canyon
Bark River-Harris	Inkster-Edison	Benson	Kingman[a]
Big Rapids	Jackson[a]	Bisbee	Mayer
Boyne Falls	Kalamazoo[b]	Camp Verde	Page
Buena Vista	Kenowa Hills	Cave Creek	Phoenix[b]
Caledonia	Kentwood[a]	Chinle	Pima
Charlevoix	Lansing[b]	Chino Valley	Prescott
Coldwater	Mount Pleasant	Clarkdale	Queen Creek
Detroit[b]	Oak Park	Concho	Safford
Elk Rapids	Onekama	Coolidge	Saint Johns
Flat Rock	Pentwater	Cottonwood	Scottsdale[b]
Forest Hills[a]	Petoskey	Enrenberg	Sedona
Godwin Heights	Sault Sainte Marie	Flagstaff[a]	Show Low
Grand Blanc[a]	Southfield[a]	Fountain Hills	Sierra Vista
Hartland	Wayne-Westland[b]	Gilbert[a]	Tempe[b]
Hillsdale	Westwood	Globe	Tuba City
Holland[a]	Wyoming[a]	Golden Valley	Vail
		Green Valley	Winslow
		Higley	

[a]Indicates a large city district (enrollment in one grade between 500 and 1,000).

[b]Indicates a very large city district (enrollment in one grade typically more than 1,000).

Sources: Michigan Department of Education (2000 various) and Arizona Department of Education (2000 various).

Note: The share of students who live in a district and attend charter schools is difficult to calculate because students can attend charter schools located outside of their districts (Michigan) or municipality (Arizona). Statistics are calculated under the assumption that students attend a charter school located in their district (Michigan) or municipality (Arizona).

local circumstances. In some cases, they may have formed where parents were unusually concerned about education and active (good circumstances for achievement). Elsewhere, charter schools may have formed where parents and teachers were frustrated because the district was poorly run (bad circumstances for achievement). Thus, it is important to look at how each school changes, subtracting its initial level of performance. I do this by allowing each school's achievement to have a fixed effect, which is simply a method of subtracting each school's initial level of performance.

Moreover, I compare Michigan schools that faced charter competition with those that did not, over the same period. Recall that Michigan enacted a school finance reform, which affected all schools, at the same time that charter schools were enacted. Thus, I am looking for changes that occurred in schools facing competition, *above and beyond* the changes that occurred in other schools in the state, which may have been responding to the finance reform.

Table 4 shows the change in achievement for schools that faced charter competition above and beyond the change in achievement for schools that faced no such competition over the same period. This statistic is sometimes called "difference-in-differences" because it contains two differences:

average of (achievement after − achievement before) in schools that faced competition

minus

average of (achievement after − achievement before) in schools that did not face competition.

The statistic should be familiar from medical experiments in which researchers subtract the change in health experienced by the control group (who receive a placebo) from the change in health experienced by the treatment group (who receive the real treatment).

TABLE 4
Effects of Charter School Competition on
Michigan Public School Students' Achievement

Difference-in-Differences Results	Dependent Var: Achievement Based on:			
Change in achievement (NPR score) after district is faced with charter school competition (charter schools represent at least 6% of enrollment in district)	Fourth-grade reading exam	Fourth-grade math exam	Seventh-grade reading exam	Seventh-grade math exam
	1.21^a	1.11^b	1.37^a	0.96^b
	(0.65)	(0.62)	(0.60)	(0.48)

[a]Change in achievement is statistically different from zero with 95% confidence.

[b]Statistically different at the 90% level.

Source: Michigan Department of Education (2000 various).

Note: The table is based on regressions of school level data from 1992–93 to 1999–2000. The dependent variable is a school's achievement—specifically, its scale scores on the Michigan Assessment of Educational Progress (MEAP) tests, which are administered to fourth and seventh graders. Regression includes school indicator variables that are constant over the period (location, neighborhood, organization) and year indicator variables that allow for statewide changes from year to year in the test itself or in the pressure to perform well. From 1992 to 2000, the means and standard deviation of average test scores (weighted by the number of test takers) were: mean of 611, standard deviation of 19 on fourth-grade reading; mean of 528, standard deviation of 16 on fourth-grade math; mean of 600, standard deviation of 17 on seventh-grade reading; mean of 521, standard deviation of 14 on seventh-grade math.

Table 4 shows difference-in-differences statistics for Michigan's fourth- and seventh-grade exams. Fourth-grade reading and math scores were, respectively, 1.21 and 1.11 scale points higher in schools that faced charter competition *after* they began to face competition. Seventh-grade reading and mathematics scores were, respectively, 1.37 and 0.96 scale points higher. Recall that these improvements in scores are relative not only to the schools' own initial performance (the first difference) but also to the gains made over the same period by Michigan schools that did not face charter competition (the difference-in-differences).[10]

In short, Michigan public schools raised achievement in the face of competition from charter schools. They raised achievement not only relative to their own previous performance but also relative to other Michigan schools not subjected to charter competition. The improvements in achievement appear to occur once charter competition reaches a critical level at which a public school should notice that a charter school is consistently drawing away students.

Michigan public schools' gains are statistically significant, and we should keep in mind that a scale point is worth between 1.25 and 2.5 percentile points. Nevertheless, the improvement in Michigan's public schools is more modest than the improvement in Milwaukee schools subjected to voucher competition. We cannot know, at this point, why the difference is more modest. It is likely that the threat of competition in Milwaukee was more serious than the threat of competition in Michigan, if for no other reason than that Milwaukee's voucher program grew much more rapidly (when it was released from enrollment constraints) than Michigan's charter schools grew. This is perhaps because Milwaukee's program had some history by 1998, whereas charter schools were truly fledglings for the first few years after Michigan's reform.

---

[10]Some readers may be interested in detrended difference-in-differences results—that is, estimates that allow each school to have a different initial trend. To compute such results, I look for *changes* in a school's trend when it begins to face charter competition. I present such results for Michigan in Hoxby, "School Choice and School Productivity," in Hoxby, ed., *The Economic Analysis of School Choice* (Chicago: University of Chicago Press, 2002). They simply confirm the results shown in Table 4: schools that faced charter competition improved their achievement growth rates more than schools that did not face charter competition. Detrended difference-in-differences results are a valid test of the effects of charter competition, even if schools faced with charter competition had initial achievement growth rates different from schools that were not faced with charter competition.

There may be other reasons that the results for Michigan are more modest: It is simply too early to test other explanations.

The Effect of Charter Schools on
Arizona Public School Students

Like Michigan, Arizona enacted a charter school law in 1994. Arizona's charter school law is widely regarded as the most favorable to charter schools in the United States, because it allows them to have considerable fiscal and legal autonomy. It also places few constraints on the growth of charter schools. As a result, 5.3 percent of Arizona's nonprivate enrollment was in charter schools in 1999–2000—the highest of any American state.

In Arizona, state-sponsored charter schools get a fee equal to the state's share of revenue (45 percent of total revenue for a regular public school). District-sponsored charter schools get a fee equal to local per pupil revenue but are less able to compete with the regular public schools because they must seek renewal of their charters from the very districts with which they compete.

My evaluation of Arizona follows the same strategy that I employ for Michigan, so I will merely highlight a few differences between the two situations. In Arizona, a municipality may contain multiple districts: for instance, a few elementary districts, a middle school district, and a high school district. A local charter school may therefore be competing with multiple districts. Therefore, I associate regular public schools and charter schools with a municipality, not a district. All Arizona fourth and seventh graders were required to take the Iowa Test of Basic Skills (ITBS) through 1995–96 and have been required to take the Stanford 9 test since then. The shift in the test does not pose problems for the analysis because both tests offer national percentile rank (NPR) scores (which have a 0.97 correlation at the school level), and all the schools switched tests in the same year. Thus, it is a simple matter to use the two tests and allow for a one-time statewide shift in each national percentile rank.[11] I use NPR scores at the school level for the school years 1992–93 to 1999–2000. In order for the results in Michigan and Arizona to be as comparable as possible, I again use the same critical level—6 percent—that I use for Michigan in evaluating the level of charter schools as a competitive threat. However, a variety of critical levels between 6 percent and 11 percent produce similar results for Arizona.[12]

The right-hand panel of Table 3 lists the Arizona municipalities that had at least 6 percent of local enrollment in charter schools. Municipalities of all sizes are represented. The list includes some Arizona's largest cities (Phoenix, Tempe, Scottsdale), some medium-sized cities (Avondale, Flagstaff, Gilbert, Kingman), and 30 smaller municipalities.

As in Michigan, it is important to subtract out each Arizona school's initial achievement. Also, it is important that the difference-in-differences statistics control for what was happening to other Arizona schools over the same period. Although Arizona did not experience a school finance reform, it did have an activist state department of education that enacted numerous programs (including a school report card program so that parents would be better informed about performance).

Table 5 shows the results of the evaluation of Arizona's charter competition. The difference-in-differences statistics suggest that Arizona public schools raised achievement in response to competition from charter schools. Achievement

---

[11]To be precise, I allow for a one-time statewide shift in each percentile rank. The shifts are very small, however. The information on Arizona charter schools and all the data on Arizona schools are taken from the Arizona Department of Education (Phoenix, 2000): *Arizona Educational Directory,* electronic files, 2000; *Arizona Pupil Achievement Testing, Statewide Report,* 1988 through 1995 editions; *Average Daily Membership and Average Daily Attendance Records,* 1988 through 2000 editions; *School Report Card Program,* 1996 through 2000 editions, electronic PDF files and spreadsheet files.

[12]These results and descriptive statistics for the Arizona data set are available from the author. Choosing a level much higher than 11 percent makes the results depend unduly on just a few districts, simply because only a few districts ever face more than an 11 percent drawing away of their students.

Effects of Charter School Competition on
Arizona Public School Students' Achievement

Difference-in-Differences Results	*Dependent Var: Achievement Based on:*			
Change in achievement (NPR score) after district is faced with charter school competition (charter schools represent	*Fourth-grade reading exam*	*Fourth-grade math exam*	*Seventh-grade reading exam*	*Seventh-grade math exam*
at least 6% of enrollment in district)	2.31[a] (0.69)	2.68[a] (0.79)	1.11 (0.95)	1.59[b] (0.89)

[a]Change in achievement is statistically significantly different from zero with 95% confidence.

[b]Significantly different at the 90% level.

Source: Arizona Department of Education (1996, 1997, 1998, 1999, 2000 various).

Note: The table is based on regressions of school-level data from 1992–93 to 1999–2000. The dependent variable is a school's achievement—specifically, a school's national percentile rank (NPR) score on a nationally normed standardized test (Iowa Test of Basic Skills or the Stanford 9). Regression includes school indicator variables that are constant over the period (location, neighborhood, organization) and year indicator variables that allow for statewide changes from year to year in the test itself or in the pressure to perform on the test.

rose by 2.31 NPR points on the fourth-grade reading exam, by 2.68 NPR points on the fourth-grade math exam, and by 1.59 points on the seventh-grade math exam. (The effect on seventh-grade reading scores appears to have been positive, but it is not statistically significantly different from zero.) Recall that these gains are not only relative to the schools' own initial performance (the first difference) but are also relative to the gains made over the same by Arizona schools that did not face charter competition (the difference-in-differences).[13]

---

[13]Some readers may be interested in detrended difference-in-differences results— that is, estimates that allow each school to have a different initial trend. To compute such results, I look for *changes* in a school's trend when it begins to face charter competition. Results in Hoxby (2002) for Arizona confirm the results shown in Table 5: schools that faced charter competition improved their achievement growth rates more than schools that did not face charter competition. Detrended difference-in-differences results are a valid test of the effects of charter competition, even if schools faced with charter competition had different initial achievement growth rates than schools that were not faced with charter competition.

In summary, Arizona public schools raised achievement in the face of competition from charter schools, and their improvements occurred after they faced charter competition above a critical level at which we might expect them to take notice of their students being drawn away by charter schools. The Arizona gains are similar to or just a bit larger than the gains made by Michigan public school students.

What Happened in Milwaukee, Michigan, and Arizona Public Schools?

The effects of the Milwaukee voucher, Michigan charter school, and Arizona charter school programs on *public* school students all suggest that the efficiency response to competition swamps cream-skimming effects (if any) that choice introduces. Moreover, not only does one effect swamp the other for the average public school student, it is likely to do so for even the public school student who is most harmed by choice. Consider the following highly pessimistic and unlikely scenario: Suppose that, prior to choice, a student was in a Milwaukee school where the average student scored at the 90th percentile for Milwaukee elementary schools. Suppose that, because of choice, all of his good peers left and he remained in a public school with peers who scored, on average, at the 10th percentile for Milwaukee elementary schools. In Milwaukee, on the math exam, the difference between elementary schools at the 90th and 10th percentiles is about 32 NPR points. This means that the Milwaukee student's worst-case scenario would be to experience a fall of about 32 national percentile points in his peer group. Moreover—to make an extreme assumption—let us say that the student is so much influenced by his peers that his scores fall by 32 points. This scenario is not strictly impossible, but it is so pessimistic that it is barely plausible. Nevertheless, if the student enjoys the achievement growth rates that Milwaukee students are enjoying now in schools that face significant competition from vouchers, he will "grow out of" the bad peer effects within four-and-a-half years—that is, he will be better off for having experienced vouchers within five years of the voucher program affecting his school and peer group.

At the outset of this chapter, I noted that commentators on the subject of school choice are obsessed with the possibility that choice schools will "cream skim" from the public schools, not do the reverse; it even seems odd to raise the possibility of reverse cream skimming. Nevertheless, given that Milwaukee public school students are *positively* affected by choice, one might worry that the effects are due to reverse cream skimming. It is, however, easy to show that the effects of choice on public school students cannot be largely the result of reverse cream skimming. There are simply too few students changing schools to affect average test scores to the degree they in fact were affected. Between 1996–97 and 1999–2000, the Milwaukee public schools lost no more than 498 fourth graders to voucher schools. (The actual number is smaller because 498 is the total increase in vouchers for fourth graders, and some of the vouchers went to students who had been attending private schools, not Milwaukee public schools.) Witte, Steer, and Thorn (1995) inform us that disappointed voucher applicants (applicants who lost the lottery and therefore remained in the Milwaukee public schools) scored 5.6 points lower in reading and 10.2 points lower in math than the average Milwaukee student. They also show that voucher applicants performed at about the same level as other low-income Milwaukee students who were eligible for the vouchers.[14] If we assume that the departing voucher students were like the disappointed applicants, then their departure would raise fourth-grade scores in Milwaukee public schools by at most 0.4 points in reading and 0.8 points in math between 1996–97 and 1999–2000. These gains would imply an annual improvement of 0.14 points in reading and 0.26 points in math. Compare such improvements with 1.3 points in reading and 1.8 points in math, which are the actual annual gains of Milwaukee

[14]See John F. Witte, Troy D. Sterr, and Christopher A. Thorn, "Fifth-year Report: Milwaukee Parental Choice Program" (University of Wisconsin–Madison, Robert La Follette Institute of Public Affairs, 1995).

public school students, above and beyond the gains recorded by the control students in non-Milwaukee schools. (You can obtain the just-quoted numbers from Table 2, once you know that there were 2,376 students in schools facing more competition and 4,554 in schools facing less competition.) In short, the change in Milwaukee scores that could plausibly be caused by reverse cream skimming is an order of magnitude too small to account for the actual change in Milwaukee scores.

No scores are available for disappointed charter applicants in Michigan and Arizona, but I can compare the demographics of charter school students and regular public school students. Tables 6 and 7 show each district (Michigan) and municipality (Arizona) that has some charter school students and a total enrollment (public plus charter) of at least 1,000 students. Within each district or municipality, charter schools and public schools are compared on the shares of their students who are black and Hispanic. All the statistics are for the 1999–2000 school year.

Table 6 shows that Michigan charter schools do not cream skim or reverse cream skim in any consistent way. In the ten largest districts, for instance, some charter schools enroll a higher share of black students, some charter schools enroll a smaller share of black students, and some charter schools enroll a virtually identical share of black students as the regular public schools do. In the ten next largest districts, there is a similar lack of pattern. I should note that the black student shares are the most informative for Michigan because the state does not have many Hispanic students.

The Hispanic student shares are the most informative for Arizona because the state does not have many black students. Looking at the Hispanic share columns in Table 7, we see that charter schools appear to be very similar to the public schools with which they compete. In most cases, the charter schools' and regular public schools' shares of Hispanic students differ by only a few percent. Moreover, there is no consistent pattern to the differences that do exist. In short, the data suggest that cream skimming and reverse cream skimming are not important phenomena in Michigan and Arizona.

TABLE 6
The Demographics of Michigan's Regular
Public and Charter School Students

District	Pupils in District	%Black in Charter Schools	%Black in Public Schools	%Hispanic in Charter Schools	%Hispanic in Public Schools
Detroit	168,118	90	91	4	4
Utica	27,038	8	1	3	1
Grand Rapids	25,648	49	44	4	18
Flint	24,411	75	74	1	2
Lansing	19,461	60	35	8	14
Ann Arbor	17,113	14	17	3	3
Dearborn	16,990	30	2	3	2
Wayne-Westland	15,128	81	15	2	2
Warren	14,513	26	2	0	1
Saginaw City	13,418	38	59	14	13
Pontiac	13,138	65	62	7	12
Kalamazoo	12,191	49	44	3	6
Port Huron	12,096	6	8	3	3
Chippewa Valley	11,931	3	1	0	1
Farmington	11,671	7	7	0	1
Southfield	10,856	81	80	0	1
Midland	9,786	3	2	3	2
Kentwood	8,899	18	18	4	5
Portage	8,701	10	5	2	2
Forest Hills	8,401	4	2	3	1
Jackson	8,055	21	34	2	3
Battle Creek	8,012	12	36	3	5
Lapeer	7,724	0	0	4	2
West Ottawa	7,552	3	3	10	12
Howell	7,220	0	0	0	0
Muskegon	6,905	76	50	9	8
Grand Blanc	6,656	12	8	2	1
Roseville	6,382	23	4	1	1

TABLE 6 *(continued)*

District	Pupils in District	%Black in Charter Schools	%Black in Public Schools	%Hispanic in Charter Schools	%Hispanic in Public Schools
Van Buren	6,316	81	23	0	1
Grand Haven	6,158	0	1	0	3
Wyoming	6,124	6	8	4	10
Holland	6,085	4	5	23	32
Benton Harbor	6,044	27	92	6	1
Bedford	5,611	1	0	1	2
Carman-Ainsworth	5,428	36	20	6	2
Saginaw	4,935	63	7	10	6
Ferndale	4,893	83	33	0	1
Holly	4,622	0	2	1	2
Hartland	4,606	1	1	0	1
Romulus	4,510	4	45	1	1
Mount Pleasant	4,407	2	2	2	3
Southgate	4,354	8	2	12	4
Kenowa Hills	4,147	6	2	5	3
Oak Park	4,107	100	84	0	0
Greenville	4,008	0	0	4	2
Highland Park	3,915	100	100	0	0
Coldwater	3,686	1	1	6	2
Inkster	3,607	90	98	0	0
Eaton Rapids	3,448	0	1	2	2
Lakeview (Calhoun)	3,381	14	4	6	2
Waverly	3,373	25	17	5	7
Sault Sainte Marie	3,315	0	0	0	0
Cedar Springs	3,273	0	0	3	2
Petoskey	3,253	1	1	1	1
Byron Center	2,905	2	1	1	2
Huron	2,677	4	1	2	2
Big Rapids	2,622	5	6	2	1
Godwin Heights	2,560	52	10	13	15

TABLE 6 (continued)

District	Pupils in District	%Black in Charter Schools	%Black in Public Schools	%Hispanic in Charter Schools	%Hispanic in Public Schools
Belding	2,503	0	0	0	1
Comstock Park	2,379	2	5	3	3
Hillsdale	2,234	1	0	2	1
Spring Lake	2,230	0	0	0	1
Buena Vista	2,046	88	90	6	6
Essexville-Hampton	2,007	5	1	14	2
Beaverton	1,842	2	1	0	1
Tawas	1,813	7	0	0	0
Manistee	1,802	3	1	7	3
Elk Rapids	1,737	1	0	3	5
Fennville	1,730	0	2	7	33
Leslie	1,495	0	0	0	2
Westwood Heights	1,463	64	57	2	3
Charlevoix	1,460	1	1	0	2
Atherton	1,270	10	4	4	2
Ishpeming	1,168	0	0	0	0

TABLE 7
The Demographics of Arizona's Regular Public and Charter School Students

	Pupils in City	%Black in Charter Schools	%Black in Public Schools	%Hispanic in Charter Schools	%Hispanic in Public Schools
Phoenix	206,773	16	7	40	46
Tucson	122,375	8	5	35	41
Mesa	74,134	4	3	19	21
Glendale	50,427	12	5	22	24
Scottsdale	33,926	4	2	9	7
Chandler	30,159	5	5	12	25
Gilbert	25,336	3	3	7	11
Yuma	23,253	3	3	69	64
Tempe	22,740	17	8	32	29

TABLE 7 *(continued)*

	Pupils in City	%Black in Charter Schools	%Black in Public Schools	%Hispanic in Charter Schools	%Hispanic in Public Schools
Peoria	20,769	6	4	26	20
Flagstaff	12,214	3	2	11	16
Casa Grande	8,085	2	5	42	46
Kingman	7,745	0	1	6	10
Avondale	7,220	12	7	35	45
Sierra Vista	7,015	12	11	24	22
Nogales	6,536	0	0	99	98
Apache Junction	6,013	1	1	10	12
Lake Havasu City	5,987	1	1	18	13
Prescott	5,643	0	1	8	9
Bullhead City	5,523	1	2	2	28
Douglas	4,722	0	2	100	89
Show Low	4,465	4	1	6	8
Cave Creek	4,230	2	1	4	5
Cottonwood	3,463	4	1	12	19
Page	3,446	1	0	5	2
Safford	3,272	2	3	32	41
Chino Valley	2,781	0	0	4	10
Globe	2,723	2	0	49	27
San Luis	2,220	0	0	100	100
Fountain Hills	2,214	1	1	7	4
Queen Creek	2,205	0	0	8	40
Somerton	1,993	0	0	100	94
Marana	1,914	0	2	9	27
Camp Verde	1,654	1	0	3	14
Willcox	1,639	0	0	27	42
Sedona	1,595	3	0	8	14
Higley	1,435	3	2	3	13
Benson	1,223	2	1	17	24
Bisbee	1,103	0	0	42	53

THE EFFECT OF TRADITIONAL FORMS OF SCHOOL CHOICE ON PUBLIC SCHOOL STUDENTS

Parents' ability to choose among public school districts (through residential decisions) and to choose private schools are such established features of American education that they are taken for granted. Yet, through these mechanisms, American parents have traditionally exercised some choice over their children's schooling. These traditional forms of choice are useful for establishing the effects of choice on achievement, especially because the availability of traditional choice mechanisms varies greatly across metropolitan areas in the United States. Some metropolitan areas contain many independent school districts and a large number of affordable private schools; others are completely monopolized by one school district or have almost no private schooling.

In previous work, I have drawn upon traditional forms of choice to generate evidence about how choice affects achievement. I review this evidence here.[15] Traditional forms of choice generate evidence that is useful because it is *long-run* and *general*—that is, traditional choice can affect all schools, not just selected schools; and can affect schools for decades.

In the short term, an administrator who is attempting to raise achievement has only certain options. He can induce his staff to work harder; he can get rid of unproductive staff and programs; he can allocate resources away from non-achievement-oriented activities (building self-esteem) and toward achievement-oriented ones (math, reading, and so on). In the slightly longer term, he can renegotiate the teacher contract to make the school more efficient. If an administrator actually pursues all these options, he may be able to raise achievement substantially.

---

[15]For detail on the empirical work described here, see Hoxby, "Do Private Schools Provide Competition for Public Schools?" revision of National Bureau of Economic Research Working Paper no. 4978, August 2000; and Hoxby, "Does Competition Among Public Schools Benefit Students and Taxpayers?" *American Economic Review* 90, no. 5 (2000): 1209–38.

Nevertheless, choice can affect achievement through a variety of long-term, general mechanisms that are not immediately available to an administrator. The financial pressures of choice may bid up the wages of teachers whose teaching raises achievement and attracts parents. In this way it may draw people into teaching (or keep people in teaching) who would otherwise pursue other careers. Indeed, it may change the entire structure of rewards in teaching and thereby transform the profession.[16] The need to attract parents may force schools to issue more information about their achievement, thus gradually making parents better "consumers." Because parents' decisions are more meaningful when schools are financed by fees they control, choice may make schools more receptive to parent participation. The need to produce results that are competitive with those of other schools may force schools to recognize and abandon pedagogical techniques and curricula that are unsuccessful in practice though philosophically appealing. Finally, in the long term, choice can affect the size and very existence of schools. Choice makes enrollment expand and contract; it makes private schools enter and exit. In the short term, we mainly observe how the existing stock of schools changes its behavior.

Both traditional forms of choice can inform us about the long-run, general effects of choice on achievement.

Traditional Inter-District Choice

The first traditional form of choice occurs when parents choose among independent public school districts by deciding where to live. Of course, the extent to which parents can exercise this form of choice depends on the number, size, and housing patterns of districts in the area of the parents' jobs. There are some metropolitan areas in the United States that have many small school districts with reasonably comparable char-

---

[16]For more on this point, see Hoxby. "Would School Choice Change the Teaching Profession?" *Journal of Human Resources* (forthcoming; also NBER Working Paper no. 7866, August 2000).

acteristics: Boston, for instance, has 70 school districts within a 30-minute commute of the downtown area and many more in the metropolitan area. Miami, on the other hand, has only one school district (Dade County) that covers the entire metropolitan area. Most metropolitan areas are, of course, somewhere between these two extremes. A typical metropolitan area has an amount of choice that corresponds to having four equal-sized school districts (or a greater number of less equally sized districts).[17] For this traditional form of choice to be a useful guide to the productivity effects of choice, parents must choose districts that are fiscally and legally independent. This is because the mechanism by which parents' housing choices translate into budgetary incentives for a school to be productive does not operate if, say, a district relies entirely on state revenue or is otherwise held harmless from repercussions associated with an inability to attract parents.

How does one measure the degree of traditional inter-district choice in a metropolitan area? A particularly good index of inter-district choice is the probability that, in a random encounter, two students in the same metropolitan area would be enrolled in different school districts. If there were only one district, as in Miami, this probability would be equal to zero. If there were many districts, as in Boston, this probability would be very close to one (greater than 0.95).[18] It is interesting to note that metropolitan areas as disparate as Saint Louis and Seattle have comparably high degrees of inter-district choice. Metropolitan areas as disparate as Las Vegas and Wilmington equally have zero inter-district choice.

---

[17]People with jobs in rural areas typically have only one or two school districts among which to choose. In order to avoid a much-choice/little-choice comparison that mainly reflects urban/rural difference in school productivity, it is useful to focus on metropolitan areas when analyzing traditional inter-district choice.

[18]We can calculate this choice index, C_m, using the following equation:

$$C_m = 1 - \sum_{j=1}^{J} s_{jm}^2 \,,$$

where s_{jm}^2 is the square of district j's share of enrollment in metropolitan area m.

Notwithstanding the range of metropolitan areas with less choice and the range of metropolitan areas with more choice, it is a good idea to control for background variables that might affect achievement: household income, parents' educational attainment, family size, single-parent households, race, region, metropolitan area size, and the local population's income, racial composition, poverty, educational attainment, and urbanness. Because I have good measures of racial, ethnic, and income segregation by school and school district, I also control for segregation that may be affected by inter-district choice. I also instrument for the measure of inter-district choice with factors that are likely to affect only the supply of districts, not the demand for them.[19]

The evidence on traditional choice among districts is shown in Table 8, which displays only the effects that are of primary interest, not the effects of control variables. The estimates show that inter-district choice has a positive, statistically significant effect on achievement. In particular, a metropolitan area with maximum inter-district choice (index approximately equal to one) has eighth-grade reading scores that are 3.8 national percentile points higher, tenth-grade math scores that are 3.1 national percentile points higher, and twelfth-grade reading scores that are 5.8 national percentile points higher.

---

[19]Although this is an issue that may interest only a few readers, we might be concerned that the conduct of local public schools affects the availability of inter-district choice. In particular, districts might consolidate with good districts but secede from bad districts. To obtain unbiased estimates, we need geographic factors that increase a metropolitan area's tendency to contain many independent districts but have no direct effect on contemporary public school conduct. As explained in Hoxby, "Does Competition Among Public Schools Benefit Students and Taxpayers?" streams and rivers are such factors because, early in American history, they were natural barriers that influenced the drawing of district boundaries. To lessen travel time to school, school districts were drawn smaller. Today, small streams and rivers probably have no direct effect on how schools conduct themselves.

TABLE 8
Effect of Traditional Inter-District Choice
on *Public* School Students' Achievement

Effect on Achievement	*8th-grade reading score*	*10th-grade math score*	*12th-grade reading score*
An increase of 1% in the index of inter-district choice (no choice to maximum choice) changes achievement by this many national percentile points in a metropolitian area	3.818[a] (1.591)	3.061[a] (1.494)	5.770[a] (2.208)

[a]Effect is statistically significantly different from zero at the 95% level of confidence.

Source: Hoxby, "Does Competition Among Public Schools Benefit Students and Taxpayers?" *American Economic Review* 90, no. 5 (2000): 1209–38. Observations are metropolitan area students from the National Education Longitudinal Study. Number of observations in each column: 10,790 (211 metropolitan areas), 7,776 (211 metropolitan areas), and 6,119 (209 metropolitan areas). Number of observations varies due to the availability of the dependent variable. See also *School District Data Book, Common Core of Data, City and County Data Book,* Geographic Names Information System, and United States Geographic Survey.

Note: Test scores are measured in national percentile points. The coefficients shown come from instrumental variables' estimation of regressions in which the dependent variable is one of the achievement measures shown on per pupil spending. The independent variables in the regression include the index of choice (instrumented by a vector of streams variables), several family background variables (household income, gender, race, parents' education), several neighborhood variables (mean household income in district, income inequality in district, racial composition of district, racial and ethnic homogeneity of district, educational attainment of adults in district), and several characteristics of the metropolitan area (population, land area, mean household income, income inequality, racial composition, racial homogeneity, ethnic homogeneity, educational attainment of adults, homogeneity of educational attainment, region of the country). Regressions are weighted by school enrollment. Standard errors are in parentheses and use formulas [Brent Moulton, "Random Group Effects and the Precision of Regression Estimates," *Journal of Econometrics* 32 (1986): 385–97] for data grouped by districts and metropolitan areas.

Traditional Choice of Private Schools

The second way in which parents have traditionally been able to exercise choice in the United States is by enrolling their children in private schools. Traditionally, private school tuition in America is not subsidized by public funds (as it is in Canada and many European countries), so parents can only afford private school if they can pay tuition and also pay taxes to support local public schools. Partly as a result, private schools enroll only 12 percent of American students.

In the United States, 85 percent of private school students attend a school with religious affiliation, but such schools include a variety of Christian and non-Christian schools and have tuition that ranges from a token amount to over $10,000. The remaining 15 percent of private school students attend schools with no religious affiliation; these include most of the independent, college-preparatory schools that charge tuition of $5,000 or more. The modal private school student in the United States attends a Catholic school that charges between $1,200 and $2,700.

A key feature of American private schools is that they typically subsidize tuition with revenues from donations or an endowment (or implicit revenues from an in-kind endowment such as buildings and land). The share of schooling cost that is covered by subsidies is larger in schools that serve low-income students, but even relatively expensive private schools charge subsidized tuition. For instance, Catholic elementary schools, on average, cover 50 percent of their costs with nontuition revenues.

The number of private school places (of a given quality) that are available at a given tuition varies greatly among metropolitan areas in the United States.[20] For instance, in some metro-

---

[20]The quality of a private school can be measured in various ways, the simplest of which is simply the amount of money the school spends on educating a student. Because private schools face strong incentives to be productive, their costs are a good guide to their quality. Private school expenditure sometimes understates the true cost of educating a student because, especially in schools with religious affiliation, labor is donated by volunteers and church buildings are used for educational purposes.

politan areas, 15 percent of the elementary student population is enrolled in private schools where tuition is about two-thirds of the schools' per pupil expenditure. (Typical amounts would be tuition of $1,800 and expenditure of about $2,700.) In other metropolitan areas, fewer than one percent of the elementary school population is enrolled in such schools, although places might be available in schools where tuition is higher because there are no tuition subsidies. In short, the supply of private schooling varies among metropolitan areas, and—thus—the degree to which parents have choice between public and private schools varies among metropolitan areas.

It is reasonable to use the actual share of students who attend private school in a metropolitan area as a measure of private school availability *if* the measure is instrumented by factors that affect the supply of private schooling rather than by factors that affect the demand for private schooling (such as the low quality of local public schools). The best instruments come from historical differences in the religious composition of metropolitan areas. Briefly, religious groups left endowments that today generate differences in the amount of nontuition revenue enjoyed by private schools. A private school presented by history with a generous endowment can provide a given quality of schooling at a lower tuition, which accordingly makes it more competitive with public schools than a private school with little or no endowment.[21]

Table 9 shows the results of greater availability of private schools. The estimates control for the same background variables that I used for inter-district choice (see above). The table shows that private school choice has a positive, statistically significant effect on *public* school students' achievement. For instance, compare two metropolitan areas, one

---

[21]Formally, the set of instruments for the share of enrollment in private schools is a vector of variables that measure the population densities of nine major religious denominations in 1950. So long as I control for *current* religious composition of metropolitan areas (which might affect the demand for private schooling), these historical religious population densities should mainly affect the supply of schooling and should have little or no direct effect on the achievement of public school students.

TABLE 9

Effect of Traditional Private School Choice
on *Public* School Students' Achievement

Effect on Achievement	8th-grade *reading score*	8th-grade *math score*	12th-grade *reading score*	12th-grade *math score*
An increase of 1% in the the share of students who attend private school changes achievement by this many national percentile points in a metropolitan area	0.271[a] (0.090)	0.249[a] (0.090)	0.342[a] (0.172)	0.371[a] (0.171)

[a]Effect is statistically significantly different from zero at the 95% level of confidence.

Source: Hoxby, "Do Private Schools Provide Competition for Public Schools?" Revision of NBER Working paper no. 4978, August 2000. Observations are metropolitan area students from the National Education Longitudinal Study. See also *School District Data Book, Common Core of Data,* and *City and County Data Book.*

Note: Test scores are measured in national percentile points. The coefficients shown come from instrumental variables' estimation of regressions in which the dependent variable is one of the achievement measures shown. The independent variables in the regression include the percentage of metropolitan area students enrolled in private schools (instrumented by a vector of religious composition variables from 1950), several family background variables (household income, gender, race, parents' education), several neighborhood variables (mean household income in district, income inequality in district, racial composition of district, racial and ethnic homogeneity of district, educational attainment of adults in district), and several characteristics of the metropolitan area (population, land area, mean household income, income inequality, racial composition, racial homogeneity, ethnic homogeneity, educational attainment of adults, homogeneity of educational attainment, region of the country). Regressions are weighted by school enrollment. Standard errors are in parentheses and use formulas (Moulton 1986) for data grouped by districts and metropolitan areas.

with a moderately high degree of private school supply (about 17 percent of students in private schools) and the other with a moderately low degree of private school supply (about 7 percent of students in private schools). The difference between moderately high and low private school choice is, thus, a 10 percentage point difference in the share of students in private schools. This means that we can interpret the coefficient shown in Table 9 as follows: A *public* school in the metropolitan area with moderately high private school choice (as opposed to moderately low private school choice) has eighth-grade reading scores that are 2.7 national percentile points higher, eighth-grade math scores that are 2.5 national percentile points higher, twelfth-grade reading scores that are 3.4 national percentile points higher, and twelfth-grade math scores that are 3.7 national percentile points higher.

Discussion of the Effects of Traditional Forms of School Choice

One should keep in mind that both traditional forms of choice provide rather weak incentives compared with choice reforms like vouchers and charter schools. Moreover, many poor families cannot exercise either traditional form of choice. A family can only choose among districts if it can afford to live in a variety of areas, and a family can only exercise traditional private school choice if it can pay tuition. Thus, even if every metropolitan area in the United States had the maximum degree of the traditional forms of choice, poor families would probably be left with schools that did not aggressively pursue achievement.

CONCLUSIONS

In this chapter, I have presented evidence that suggests that the school choice debate should focus much more on how *public* schools respond to competition. It appears that public schools are induced to raise achievement when they are faced with competition and that this stimulus swamps any effect associated with cream skimming, reverse cream skimming, or the like. The choice reforms that are currently in place do not appear to generate both winners and losers— only winners. *Public* school students, who are often predicted to be losers, are winners because their schools apparently respond positively to competitive threats. This is not only good news for students; it should be welcome news to those who think that public schools have much good potential that is brought out only when need arises.

7

The Structure of School Choice

Terry M. Moe

A common argument against school choice is that it leads to equity problems. When parents are given the right to choose, critics argue, children who are already advantaged—with better educated, more motivated, higher income parents—are the ones who reap the rewards of new educational opportunities, while poor and minority children are left behind in the regular public schools—schools that, because of the outflow of good students and much-needed resources, are even less capable of serving them.[1]

This is a troubling argument that deserves to be taken seriously. If true, it implies that an expansion of parental choice may worsen problems of class and race that our nation has been struggling for decades to overcome, a prospect most Americans would probably regard as convincing reason for rejecting choice as a major avenue of reform. If it is not true, however—because these sorts of problems can be addressed and mitigated, or because choice can actually

---

[1]See, e.g.: Bruce Fuller and Richard Elmore, and Gary Oldfield, eds., *Who Chooses? Who Loses?* (New York: Teachers College Press, 1996); Peter W. Cookson, Jr., *School Choice: The Struggle for the Soul of American Education* (New Haven, Conn.: Yale University Press, 1994); and Amy Stuart Wells, *Time to Choose: America at the Crossroads of School Choice Policy* (New York: Hill and Wang, 1993).

serve as a mechanism for promoting social equity—then the case for choice would obviously be far more attractive.

Which of these several possibilities is correct? The answer is that they can each be correct, depending on how choice programs are designed. The simple way to think of it is that school choice always operates within a structure—a framework of rules—which in turn has a lot to do with the kinds of outcomes choice will ultimately generate. In some structures, choice will lead to equity problems. In others, it will not. In still others, it will tilt the playing field in favor of the disadvantaged and aggressively promote the cause of social equity.

The debate over school choice almost always consists of simplified claims that fail to recognize the key role of structure. Participants are well aware that there are different kinds of choice, from vouchers to charter schools to magnet schools, and that different rules apply to each. But beyond these broad categories, much of the public debate is generic and structure-free. Even academics find themselves talking about whether vouchers promote academic achievement, or whether charter schools have competitive effects on regular public schools, without recognizing that these and other types of choice can all be structured in very different ways, leading to very different outcomes, and that it usually makes little sense to ask whether vouchers or charter schools, in some generic sense, have particular effects. Their effects depend on the specific structures in which they are embedded, and they can only be understood and evaluated in that way.

Precisely because this is so, the great challenge for educational reformers—and the great opportunity—is to choose the right structures. With the right structures, the problems sometimes associated with choice can be minimized or reversed, and the power of markets can be harnessed for the promotion of important social values. As a practical matter, of course, decisions about structure get made through the political process; and politics being what it is, there is no guarantee that those structures judged best on analytical grounds will actually get adopted. Still, opportunities abound for making good decisions about structure, and for using markets to social advantage within the education system.

My aim in this chapter, then, is to highlight two simple topics that lie at the heart of the choice issue but are only rarely the subject of serious discussion or study. The first has to do with the structure of choice. The second has to do with the choice of structure. These are the keys to understanding the role of choice in American education.

THE ECONOMY, STRUCTURE, AND THE FREE MARKET

A voucher system for American education was first proposed in 1955 by Milton Friedman, a libertarian economist whose contributions to economic theory and social policy have made him one of the most influential thinkers of the last century. Friedman's best-known statement of the case for vouchers can be found in his book, *Capitalism and Freedom* (1962). Friedman and other libertarians believe that when markets are allowed to work freely with a minimum of government interference, society will be maximally productive and efficient.[2]

It is tempting to imagine that the free market is without structure, unconstrained by an overarching set of governmental rules. But even libertarians don't see it this way. They recognize that, for markets to work properly, a society needs to have well-defined property rights backed by a legal system that enforces contracts and the rule of law. These are structures imposed by government. It is not markets alone, but markets embedded in such a governmental structure, that yield the wondrous results they ascribe to the free market.

---

[2]See Milton Friedman, "The Role of Government in Education," in Robert A. Solow, ed., *Economics and the Public Interest* (New Brunswick, N.J.: Rutgers University Press); see also Milton Friedman and Rose Friedman, *Free to Choose* (New York: Avon Books, 1980).

Within education circles, there is a tendency to equate economics with the free market, and to discuss proposals for
greater choice and competition in American education as
though they are efforts to replace public education with the
free market. But this perspective on economics and market-
based reforms is unwarranted. The fact is, proportionately
few economists are proponents of truly free markets. The
vast majority would argue that, although markets are powerful means of promoting social welfare, their performance
depends on the real-world conditions under which they operate; and under some conditions, economists know, the performance of markets and the well-being of society will suffer.
This can happen, for instance, if consumers are poorly informed, if the goods in question are public goods, if competition is inherently limited, if producers can conspire to fix
prices or create monopolies, or if information-based problems of moral hazard or adverse selection undermine market
transactions.

Accordingly, much of mainstream economics is devoted
not to the study of markets per se, but to the conditions that
affect how markets work, to the problems these conditions
can produce, and to how these problems can be addressed so
that the power of markets can better promote the social
good. Economists generally agree that the solution to market
imperfections rests with an appropriately designed framework of governmental rules, a structure that imposes basic
(but not onerous) regulations on economic decisionmakers.[3]

In broad outline, at least, the reality of modern government is a reflection of this professional consensus about how
markets can best be put to use. The United States is often de-

---

[3]See David L. Weimer and Aidan R. Vining, *Policy Analysis: Concepts and Prac-
tice,* 3d ed. (Englewood Cliffs, N.J.: Prentice-Hall, 1998); Joseph E. Stiglitz, *Eco-
nomics of the Public Sector,* 3d ed. (New York: W. W. Norton, 2000); Steven E.
Rhoads, *The Economist's View of the World: Government, Markets, and Public
Policy* (New York: Cambridge University Press, 1985); Lester Thurow, *Zero-Sum
Society* (New York: Basic Books, 1980); Charles Wolf, *Markets or Governments:
Choosing Between Imperfect Alternatives* (Cambridge, Mass.: MIT Press, 1988).

scribed as the paradigmatic free-market economy. But it is actually an aggressive regulator of economic transactions along a whole host of dimensions, ranging from antitrust to environmental protection to deceptive practices to labor relations to employment discrimination to securities trading to consumer protection and more. A detailed structure of regulation, moreover, although varying in content from country to country, is typical of the way most nations in the Western world have organized their economies. The modern market economy is not in any meaningful sense a free market. It is a mixed system of government and markets in which governmental rules constrain and channel how markets work.[4]

Although economists applaud the emergence and international dominance of these mixed systems, the specific regulations that governments adopt are not always (or even usually) optimal from an analytical standpoint. The reason can be summed up in a single word: politics. Government regulations are inevitably adopted through the democratic political process, not through the analytic steering of economists, and thus are subject to influence by powerful political interests and parochial constituencies that are little concerned with what might be best for society. Because this is so, a mixed system may have regulations that are excessive, stacked in favor of special interests, and poorly designed to put markets to their most effective social uses.[5]

Most economists would no doubt prefer a simpler, less politicized regulatory structure than governments actually create. But there is not much they can do to change the nature of politics. And there is no indication that, even if they could change things, they would prefer a true free-market system to

---

[4]See, e.g., Murray L. Weidenbaum, *Business, Government, and the Public*, 3d ed. (Englewood Cliffs, N.J.: Prentice-Hall, 1986); and Charles E. Lindblom, *Politics and Markets* (New York: Basic Books, 1977).

[5]See, e.g., Wolf, *Markets or Governments*; Lindblom, *Politics and Markets*; Theodore Lowi, *The End of Liberalism: The Second Republic of the United States* (New York: W. W. Norton, 1979); Terry M. Moe, "The Politics of Bureaucratic Structure," in John E. Chubb and Paul E. Peterson, *Can the Government Govern?* (Washington, D.C.: Brookings Institution Press, 1989).

the kind of regulated system we have now. The fact is, the system we have performs remarkably well despite its flaws, and there is widespread support for it within the profession.

It is a mistake, then, for educators to see economists as proponents of free markets, and to see proposals for school choice, competition, and other market-based reforms as efforts to introduce free markets into American education. When economists and other market advocates think about education, just as when they think about the economy, the fundamental question is: how can markets be used to social advantage? In so doing, they recognize the great power of markets to promote incentives and efficiency—but they also recognize that, if markets are to promote desired social values in the most effective ways, they must often be constrained and guided by a set of social rules that are chosen with that in mind.

CHOICE WITHOUT DESIGN: THE CURRENT EDUCATION SYSTEM

From its modern origins in the early decades of the 1900s, America's public education system was designed to be a purely governmental system in which markets play no role at all. There was simply no attempt to take advantage of what markets might have to offer. Instead, the idea was that educational services would be produced by government-run schools, which would act as local monopolies within their own geographic areas. Children would be assigned to their local schools. And the schools, along with every aspect of educational policy, organization, and practice, would be democratically controlled through a complex hierarchy of political officials and educational bureaucrats.[6]

---

[6]See Andrew J. Coulson, *Market Education: The Unknown History* (New Brunswick, N.J.: Transaction Publishers, 1999); Lawrence A. Cremin, *The Transformation of the School: Progressivism in American Education, 1876–1957* (New York: Alfred A. Knopf, 1961); and David B. Tyack, *The One Best System: A History of American Urban Education* (Cambridge, Mass.: Harvard University Press, 1974).

This same top-down structure has prevailed ever since. The details have changed in many respects over the years, of course, and the choice movement has made a degree of headway. There are now four public voucher programs in operation (all of them small). There are some 2,000 charter schools, enrolling more than 500,000 kids. There are magnet schools in many urban areas. And there are programs of interdistrict and intradistrict choice. But these reforms are a drop in a very large bucket. Public education remains, as ever, a top-down system of government control.[7]

Even a purely governmental system, however, does not eliminate all forms of choice. In the case of American education, parents are typically denied the right to choose their children's public schools, but they are still free to make all sorts of other choices that affect the education of their children. In effect, there is an implicit choice system at work both inside and outside the formal governmental system. This choice system was not designed by anyone, but there is nonetheless a distinctive structure to it that shapes the way parental choices get made. And although its outcomes for society are accidental and unplanned, they are hugely important. They are also perverse, generating widespread equity problems that have worsened and entrenched the class and racial problems of American society.

The reasons are readily apparent from a brief look at the two familiar properties that, by any account, are the implicit choice system's most basic structural features.

Structure: Public school parents are (typically) not allowed to choose which public school their kids attend, but they are allowed to choose where their families will live. Operating within this rule, parents know that they can buy themselves a good public school by buying or renting a house in the right

---

[7]See Paul E. Peterson, "Choice in American Education," in Terry M. Moe, ed., *A Primer on America's Schools* (Stanford: Hoover Institution Press, 2001); and Jeffrey R. Henig and Stephen D. Sugarman, "The Nature and Extent of School Choice," in Stephen D. Sugarman and Frank R. Kemerer, eds., *School Choice and Social Controversy: Politics, Policy, and Law* (Washington, D.C.: Brookings Institution Press, 1999).

school district or neighborhood. Exercising this kind of choice is often expensive, mainly because the costs of housing in areas with good schools tend to be much higher than elsewhere (as a result of parents' bidding up the prices). Not surprisingly, then, the people who exercise residential choice tend to be those who are higher in income. They are also the ones who are most motivated by education concerns, and thus the parents who themselves are the most educated. The upshot is that residential choice injects a serious social bias into the current education system: the best schools tend to be filled with advantaged children, the worst schools with disadvantaged children. This is perhaps the most fundamental creaming problem in American education today, and the most socially destructive.[8]

Structure: *Public schools are provided free of cost by the government. Parents can choose to send their kids to private schools, but private schools are costly.* Under this rule, all parents have the option of leaving the public system and going private in search of better schools for their kids. At least in principle. But the rule also ensures that certain kinds of parents are in a far better position than others to take advantage of what the private sector has to offer. Private options are more accessible, obviously, to parents who are financially well-off. The same is true for the well educated because educated parents tend to be more motivated by educational concerns. For these reasons, the current system promotes a class bias in the types of parents who go private, which is especially apparent in school districts with the worst public schools. When public schools are performing poorly, advantaged kids flee to the private sector (and the

---

[8]For data on the social biases of residential choice, see Terry M. Moe, *Schools, Vouchers, and the American Public* (Washington, D.C.: Brookings Institution Press, 2001). For analyses of the connection between school quality and housing values, see, e.g., H. S. Rosen and D. J. Fullerton, "A Note on Local Tax Rates, Public Benefit Levels, and Property Values," *Journal of Political Economy* 85 (1977): 433–40; and G. R. Meadows, "Taxes, Spending, and Property Values: A Comment and Further Results," ibid., 84 (1976).

suburbs, via residential choice), and poor and minority kids are left behind, concentrated in schools unable to serve them. Here again, educational choices produce a creaming effect that adds to social inequities.[9]

The defenders of the public schools tend to attribute these effects to choice per se. And they argue that if more choice is introduced into the current public school system—through vouchers, say—the equity problems that plague this system will only get worse. Although the equity problems are real, it is a mistake to think that they are simply due to choice. They are actually due to the way choice happens to operate *within a particular structure*—a structure that exists because the current system of top-down control does *not* grant parents a choice of schools and makes it costly for them to exercise choice by going private.

There is great irony here. The reason choice often operates perversely within the current education system is precisely that this system was not designed to take advantage of choice, or of markets generally, but rather to keep markets out of education entirely. By trying to keep markets out, however, the system's designers unwittingly created a structure in which parental choice is a forceful influence anyway—but a perverse one (in some ways) that undermines the system's most fundamental goals.

On the Need for Choice—and Design—in Education

The Progressives who designed our education system were guided by ideas prevalent nearly a hundred years ago, when markets were not well understood and when bureaucracy and the direct governmental supply of services were regarded as innovative, even revolutionary reforms. They can be excused for building a top-down system of public education. Today, however, there is no good reason why Americans should rest content with this structural relic of

---

[9]For data on the social biases of private school choice (under the current system), see Moe, *Schools, Vouchers, and the American Public*.

the past. Its ideals—of common schooling, of social equity, of democratic governance—are inspiring. But they are poorly met in practice. If a century of theory, research, and experience has anything to teach us, it is that top-down governmental structures are extreme forms of social organization that are often overly costly and unproductive, and that, where it is practical to do so, a greater reliance on markets—which is very different, I can only reiterate, from a radical shift to free markets—makes eminently good sense and is likely to prove beneficial for society.

Why would a greater reliance on markets be good for education? Reams have been written about this, so I won't launch into an extended discussion here.[10] But two simple points, both based on the introduction of parent choice, are worth underlining.

The first point is that choice itself is valuable. It has a direct impact on families, by allowing parents to seek out better schools for their kids and improve their educational opportunities. Under the current system, they are prevented from doing this. Children are assigned to their local public school, and if that school is of poor quality or provides a kind of education families don't like, they have nowhere to go—unless they pay for the privilege of leaving. In practice, this means that parents with money can escape the trap by changing their residence or going private, but that poor parents cannot. Thus, a major advantage of choice is that it expands the opportunities of parents who are in greatest need, and who currently have little or no control over their children's educations. It also provides opportunities for parents who, on religious, moral, or pedagogical grounds, simply want a different kind of education for their children. It allows them to express and pursue their own values.

---

[10]See, e.g., John E. Chubb and Terry M. Moe, *Politics, Markets, and America's Schools* (Washington, D.C.: Brookings Institution Press, 1990); Coulson, *Market Education*; Friedman, *Capitalism and Freedom*; and John E. Coons and Stephen D. Sugarman, *Education by Choice: The Case for Family Control* (Berkeley: University of California Press, 1978).

The second point is that choice transforms incentives, and in so doing promises to transform the system as a whole. Under the current top-down arrangement, public schools are guaranteed students and resources regardless of how well they perform. The inevitable result is that they have few incentives to produce high-quality education, to respond to parents, to allocate their funds efficiently, or to innovate in socially productive ways—for nothing bad happens to them if they don't, and nothing good happens to them if they do. When parents are allowed to choose, however, the situation is very different. Parents are no longer a captive clientele, but are able to leave schools they consider undesirable and seek out schools they think are better. As a result, schools have to compete with one another for parental support, and this competition puts all schools on notice that, if they do not perform, they stand to lose students and resources to other schools that can do a better job. This gives them strong incentives to educate, to be responsive, to be efficient, to innovate. Those that respond to these incentives tend to prosper, while those that don't tend to be weeded out—leading, over time, to a more effective, more innovative population of schools.

For these and other reasons, markets have much to contribute, and the American education system could benefit were they put to wise use. Yet it would be wrong to think that markets are always beneficial and never lead to problems. To take an egregious example: during the late 1960s, "freedom of choice" plans were widely adopted in the South as a way of allowing whites to avoid going to school with blacks. This is precisely what happened: many whites used their newfound choices to seek out all-white schools, whereas the vast majority of blacks were either denied entrance or chose to avoid the risks of entering bastions of white solidarity. At that time and in that context, then, choice promoted segregation. It allowed parents the freedom to pursue their own values, a seemingly good thing, but these values happened to be racist.[11]

---

[11]See Gary Orfield, *Must We Bus? Segregated Schools and National Policy* (Washington, D.C.: Brookings Institution Press, 1978); and Wells, *Time to Choose.*

Critics argue that choice would unleash the same sorts of racist motivations today. And as they see it, race is hardly the only problem. Parents who are affluent and better educated would use the new choice opportunities to greatest advantage: abandoning the public schools, getting their kids into the best, most exclusive private schools, and leaving the poor behind. Parents would also separate themselves off by class and religion, further balkanizing our culture. And private schools would discriminate against poor and minority kids, refuse to enroll the disabled, hire unqualified teachers, offer weak programs, mislead parents with deceptive advertising, fail to socialize kids to democratic norms, and more.[12]

It is only reasonable to be concerned about these possibilities, and the critics are right to direct our attention to them. Freedom of choice plans did in fact lead to bad social consequences in the South of years ago. And there are situations in which forms of school choice have generated some of the problems the critics talk about. Studies of existing voucher programs, for example, have shown that parents who are better educated are usually the ones most likely to take advantage of choice opportunities.[13] Similarly, studies of public school choice have shown that parent choices in certain programs are often made on the basis of race or class, producing a tendency toward more segregated schools and a less equitable distribution of opportunities.[14]

---

[12]See Fuller, Elmore, and Orfield, eds., *Who Chooses? Who Loses?*; Cookson, *School Choice*; Wells, *Time to Choose.*

[13]See, e.g., John F. Witte, Troy D. Sterr, and Christopher A. Thorn, "Fifth-year Report: Milwaukee Parental Choice Program" (University of Wisconsin—Madison, Robert La Follette Institute of Public Affairs, 1995); and R. Kenneth Godwin, Frank R. Kemerer, and Valerie J. Martinez, *Final Report: San Antonio School Choice Research Project* (University of North Texas, Center for the Study of Education Reform, 1997).

[14]See, e.g., Jeffrey R. Henig, "The Local Dynamics of Choice: Ethnic Preferencesand Institutional Responses," in Fuller, Elmore, and Orfield, eds., *Who*

As extensive reviews of the research literature well demonstrate, however, the critics tend to overstate the true extent of the problems.[15] This is particularly so given that most choice programs thus far adopted (and all voucher programs) are limited entirely to poor families, and are clearly promoting social equity by giving these families—and only them—new opportunities they would not otherwise have. If there are inequities, they almost always arise because some poor families are better able to take advantage of these opportunities than other poor families are. This is regrettable (and reversible, through alternative designs), but it hardly justifies claims that these programs are somehow inequitable on the whole.

Even more important, given the central themes of this chapter, critics almost always portray these problems as somehow inherent in choice per se—and they jump to the conclusion that, with such problems therefore inevitable, reform proposals to seriously expand parental choice (and thus competition) must be opposed. What they rarely consider is that all forms of choice come with a particular structure, that some of these structures are not well designed, and that, through the conscious design of more appropriate structures, the problems they are most concerned about can be addressed and mitigated. Indeed, through appropriate design, choice plans can become vehicles by which social equity, common schooling, and other basic social values can be aggressively pursued— and far more successfully, it is reasonable to expect, than they are being pursued under the current system, which is clearly failing in these regards and is the baseline against which all reforms must be judged.

Chooses? Who Loses?; J. Douglas Willms and Frank H. Echols, "The Scottish Experience of Parental School Choice," in Edith Rasell and Richard Rothstein, eds., *School Choice: Examining the Evidence* (Washington, D.C.: Economic Policy Institute, 1993).

[15]See esp. Jeffrey R. Henig, "School Choice Outcomes," in Sugarman and Kemerer, eds., *School Choice and Social Controversy.*

The Choice of Structure

The idea of choice opens up new vistas once we recognize that a choice system can depart rather substantially from a free market, and in ways consciously designed to promote social equity and other important social values. To get a better sense of what is possible, let's take a closer look at some of the general dimensions of structure that policymakers have available to them in designing a choice system, and consider some of the options and arguments that go along with each.[16]

1. Who should qualify for a voucher? The free-market ideal is a universal voucher system in which all children qualify. Such a system would presumably extend a maximum of choice and freedom to American's families and generate beneficial competition. It may also promote social equity, because the strongest demand for vouchers and private schools comes from poor and minority families who are stuck in low-performing schools. To be sure, well-off families are likely to be better educated and informed and in better positions to take advantage of vouchers. But they are also less inclined to use them. They have already used their advantages to get good public schools, and they have little incentive to change.[17]

There are two major arguments against a universal system. The first is that it leaves equity to the uncertainties of the marketplace and cannot guarantee that disadvantaged kids (or at least some of them) will not get short shrift. Why, critics argue, should people who don't need vouchers be eligible for them in the first place? To promote equity with force and certainty, a voucher system might simply be targeted at people who are in need, starting with the neediest. When this is done, there is

---

[16]For a detailed discussion of the various elements that might make up the design of a choice system, see John E. Coons and Stephen D. Sugarman, *Making School Choice Work for All Families: A Template for Legislative and Policy Reform* (San Francisco: Pacific Research Institute, 1999).

[17]For data on the popularity of school choice among poor and minority parents, see Moe, *Schools, Vouchers, and the American Public.*

little worry that choice will lead to equity problems, because everyone who gets to choose will be poor.

The second argument—which may be persuasive even to people who favor universalism as a long-run goal—is that adopting a universal system from the get-go is too risky, involving a massive, all-at-once shift that could involve vast upheavals and uncertainties. It would be much more prudent, given the risks, to start out with small pilot programs, see how they work in practice, and move incrementally from there. If the place to start is with small pilot programs, moreover, it makes perfect sense to focus these programs on the neediest kids in society, who are poor and minority. This is where society clearly gets the most benefit, and where the risks of failure—because things are currently so bad for these kids—is exceedingly small and well worth bearing. Considerations of risk, then, just like considerations of equity, argue for programs that are targeted at the disadvantaged.

Even if targeting is preferred over universalism, though, this is not the only structural decision to be made. There are different types of targeting, and thus still other structural options to be considered and compared. In Milwaukee and Cleveland, for example, vouchers are available to children who are low in income. Florida, on the other hand, makes vouchers available to all kids who attend "failing" schools, where "failing" is defined by the schools' performance on state tests. Florida has another program, moreover, that extends vouchers to all children who qualify for special education.[18]

Each of these options has its own pluses and minuses (on which people may differ), and there is no single way to go. But the point is simply this: giving every child a voucher is just one way of designing a choice system. There are many others, and they offer a great deal of flexibility in promoting important social values.

---

[18]For information on these programs, see Robert Moffit, Jennifer Garrett, and Janice A. Smith, eds., *School Choice 2001: What's Happening in the States* (Washington, D.C.: Heritage Foundation, 2001).

2. What should the amount of the voucher be? The standard free-market solution is to give all kids vouchers of the same amount. This is simple and straightforward, whether the program is universal or targeted, and many Americans would see it as the fairest way to proceed.

But other approaches are also reasonable, especially in the context of a universal voucher program, when kids from diverse backgrounds are all getting vouchers. It is well known, for instance, that disadvantaged kids are more costly to educate than other kids are; the same is true for kids with learning disabilities, behavior problems, and other difficulties. From the standpoint of economics alone, therefore, it makes sense to give bigger vouchers to these kids than to others—both to compensate schools for the true costs of educating them, and to make these children more attractive as clients so that schools will actually compete to serve them. It also makes sense from an equity standpoint: it recognizes that children have different educational needs, and it allocates resources on that basis. This is more equitable, many would say, than "equal treatment."

As a practical matter, of course, it might be difficult to set vouchers equal to the underlying costs of education, but there are simple ways to approximate such an ideal. One way is to give all kids a base voucher, and then to "voucherize" the compensatory and special education funds currently supplied by federal and state governments, so that each child who qualifies for these programs would have additional amounts added to the base voucher. Another alternative is to have some sort of sliding scale, with the value of the vouchers being quite high for the poor, and dropping slowly and steadily until at some level of family income they become zero. These and other alternatives would have to be evaluated for their ease and cost of administration—and for whether, at least in the short run, it might make more sense simply to target vouchers solely at the poor.

However these issues are resolved, the absolute amount of the voucher is also critical. The bigger the voucher, the more schools families will be able to consider, and the more choice and opportunity they will have (particularly if they are poor). This is true from the outset, but it is especially true over the long run as the private sector has time to adjust— for the bigger the voucher, the greater the incentive for new schools to emerge, and the larger the supply of schools will ultimately be.

In Milwaukee, the voucher amount is now over $5,000 per child, which is more than enough to pay for tuition at virtually all private schools in that city, and enough to ensure that some 10,000 children have been able to attend about 100 different private schools. Yet the number of kids using the vouchers is kept lower than it otherwise would be because there is no more space in the private sector to accept additional kids, and there is little evidence that private supply is expanding to meet the new demand. Apparently, $5,000 is insufficient—especially in a climate of political uncertainty, which constantly threatens the survival of the program—to induce private schools to invest in new space, buildings, and teachers. If policymakers really want choice and competition to work for the poor, then, they may need to increase the voucher.[19]

3. Should parents be allowed to add on? The free-market solution is to allow parents to add on to their vouchers, as it simply gives parents more freedom and more choice. But the downside is that this approach might produce inequities: the more affluent parents would be better able to add their own money to the voucher in buying their way into expensive schools, leaving the poor behind to choose among the inexpensive ones, thus encouraging a two-tiered system that reinforces class cleavages.

---

[19]See Dan McKinley, "Could Private Schools Expand to Meet Demand?" in John C. Goodman and Fritz F. Steiger, *An Education Agenda: Let Parents Choose Their Children's Schools* (Dallas: National Center for Policy Analysis, 2001).

One obvious solution is for designers to adopt a rule prohibiting parents from adding on and requiring any schools participating in the program to accept the voucher as full payment. This would equalize the purchasing power of all parents who use vouchers, and it would prevent parents who insist on spending more from receiving vouchers as a subsidy. Such an approach might even be considered necessary in programs targeted solely at the poor, because even among the poor there will be some families who are better able than others to afford the extra money, and thus some families who will be left behind.

A prohibition of add-ons, then, is a reasonable structural response to the equity problem. And not surprisingly, it has been the favored approach in Milwaukee, Cleveland, and Florida. There are certain problems with it, however, that need to be recognized. It would prevent some parents, perhaps many, from choosing a school they really want for their children, and this in itself is a negative. But it would also put an upper bound on the tuition that can be charged by all schools participating in the voucher program; and unless the amount of the voucher is high, the danger is that only schools offering a basic, low-cost education could participate. A $2,000 voucher would call forth a population of $2,000 private schools, and schools wanting to offer more elaborate and costly—or simply more adequate—programs would be excluded. This would reduce variety and choice for children, as well as competition, and it would threaten to produce a population of low-performing schools. The larger the voucher, the less these problems would arise.

4. Should private schools control their own admissions? The free-market ideal is that private schools should be allowed to make their own decisions about which children to admit, based on their own criteria. But the danger exists that private schools might favor children who are easier to educate or who have more affluent parents or who are from the right religious or social group, and that poor and minority kids would not have much access to desirable schools.

This danger is worth recognizing, but it tends to be overstated. It is a mistake to think that all private schools will somehow be competing for gifted, well-behaved kids from wealthy families. Some schools may do this, but most will have to find their niches among the broader population of children and appeal to the needs and interests of ordinary families. When voucher systems are restricted to the poor, moreover, there is even less reason to worry about discrimination in admissions, as all the kids with vouchers are disadvantaged and schools cannot shunt them aside in favor of the affluent. There may, of course, be a measure of discrimination among types of poor children—in favor of those who are well behaved, for example, or who have better test scores. But the Milwaukee experience suggests that this has not been a problem in practice: low-income kids in that city use vouchers to attend nearly 100 private schools, which have so far been happy to admit them, and there have been few complaints by parents of any discrimination.

Still, the possibility of discrimination exists, even in programs for the poor. And in a universal program with a diverse population of students, some from families that are well off, the possibilities are magnified. What are the design options for dealing with them?

Two stand out. One is that, as a condition for participating in the voucher program, private schools can be required to select some portion of their students by lottery—perhaps a high portion, perhaps a low portion, depending on how serious the discrimination problem seems to be. This would ensure that poor and minority kids would have a shot at getting into the schools they prefer. A second possibility is that a certain percentage of each school's new slots can be set aside each year for low-income kids. This too would give them access to all schools, including the most desirable.

There are costs, however, to moving too aggressively in regulating private school admissions. One of the reasons many private schools are so successful is that they have the autonomy to define their own missions and programs as they see fit, and selecting appropriate students is an integral part of that. By imposing a randomly selected student body on private schools, an important foundation of their strength may be lost. Any restrictions, therefore, should be carefully considered.

5. Should private schools be held accountable by government? In a free market, private schools would not be regulated to ensure that they meet performance standards or spend their money appropriately. The idea is that such regulation would be counterproductive, violating the autonomy schools need for high performance, and that it would also be unnecessary, because in the educational marketplace private schools are automatically held accountable from below—by parents who leave bad schools, seek out better ones, and thus provide schools with the right kinds of incentives to keep them performing effectively.

Not everyone has as much faith in markets, however. This is true of many liberals, of course. But it also true of many people who have no ideological take on markets at all and are moved by very practical concerns. Government officials and taxpayers, for instance, are footing the bill for education, and they tend to want concrete assurances—not assurances derived from the theory of markets—that their money is being put to good use. They also tend to be risk-averse and worried that something could go wrong—that some private schools, for example, may offer substandard programs, or that they will indoctrinate children, or that they will steal public money.[20]

A natural response is to design rules of accountability to protect against these dangers and promote desirable outcomes. Among other things, these rules may set out requirements regarding curriculum and standards, teacher qualifications, annual audits of finances, periodic testing of students, and

---

[20]For data on public attitudes toward the regulation of voucher-receiving private schools, see Moe, *Schools, Vouchers, and the American Public.*

information about the school that must be made public. The rules may take various forms and can be as detailed as policymakers like. But because the autonomy of private schools is pivotal to their strength, and because avoiding bureaucracy and its stultifying effects is a key aim in a choice system to begin with, there are good reasons for keeping accountability regulations simple and basic, and for steering clear of heavy regulations.

6. Should religious schools be included in a voucher system? The free-market answer is that religious schools of all types should be included, as part of the general aim of providing families with the kind of education they want and giving them as much choice and diversity as possible. Polls show the American people are quite supportive of religion, and they overwhelmingly agree that, if a voucher system were to be created, religious schools should be part of it.[21] But not everyone is so disposed (especially among liberal elites). One argument is that religion should be kept out of education, particularly when it is funded with taxpayer money. A related (but quite separate) argument is that government funding of religious schools violates the "separation of church and state" and is unconstitutional. The upshot, in either case, is that only secular schools should be allowed to participate in a voucher system.

As far as the principle is concerned, people can be expected to differ on this issue. But it is important to recognize that, as a practical matter, the exclusion of religious schools has enormous consequences. Under the current system, the vast majority of private schools are religious. The reason for this is simple: public schools are offering a nonreligious education for free, and nonreligious private schools have a hard time competing with that. Religious private schools are offering something the public schools can't offer, which is why there are so many of them. With a full-blown voucher

---

[21]Ibid.

system, this would presumably change, as there would be a greater demand for nonreligious private schools—and over the long run (assuming the vouchers were big enough), there would be an increase in their supply. But in the short run, which could mean many years, most of the options in the private sector will take the form of religious schools. And if religious schools are excluded from a voucher system, there will be little for most kids to choose from. In effect, to exclude religious schools is to eliminate most choice.

7. How should government funds be divided between public and private schools? The free-market answer is that the money should follow children to their schools of choice, whether public or private. Thus, when kids leave public schools for private schools, the public schools would lose the full amount of funding for those kids, and the private schools would gain that amount. This dynamic is what produces the incentive effects of competition. It is precisely because public schools don't want to lose their money that they will have incentives to improve their performance.

Not everyone is persuaded by this line of reasoning. A standard argument—indeed, the most often recited argument against vouchers—is that they drain money out of the public schools, sapping their strength and making it even more difficult for them to improve. How can they improve with less money? A related argument is that the public schools have high fixed costs—in buildings, maintenance, administration, and the like—and cannot simply cut back on their inputs to make up for all the resources they lose when kids leave and take their total funding with them.[22]

The first of these arguments is something of a red herring. It is true that the public schools would get less money in ab-

---

[22]A corollary financial issue has to do with the budgetary impact of providing vouchers to kids who are currently in private schools. As things now stand, these kids get educated at no expense to the government. Under a voucher system, any of these kids qualifying for a voucher would require additional expense

solute terms; but this is beside the point, for they would also have fewer kids to educate. Even if the total funding followed each child, the public schools would continue to get paid for every child who stays in the public sector, and they would be paid just as much as before. The second argument is more legitimate. The public schools do have fixed costs—and especially if only a small number of kids go private (which is guaranteed if the program itself is small by design), the districts may find it difficult to achieve many cost savings. Over the long run this would change if the choice programs expand and large numbers of kids go private. But in the short run, the fixed cost issue is real.

One response is to design a system that would not allow full funding to follow the children who go private. Instead, a portion of the funding would be held back and given to the public schools. The public schools would thereby get paid for children they are not responsible for educating, but the money would make up for fixed costs that the districts must still incur after the children leave. Some policymakers may want to go further than this in holding money back for the public schools. They may reason that, once fixed costs are taken care of, the schools need additional money to ensure that they will be able to improve and meet the new competition. A market advocate would argue that

by the government, and thus—it would seem—bigger education budgets (and more taxes to pay for them). Two factors mitigate this problem. The first is that, because the voucher is usually much smaller than average per-pupil spending by the public schools, the government may save money when children switch from public to private; and if enough kids switch, the surplus may more than cover the private students who were not previously being funded. The second factor is that virtually all voucher plans being proposed these days focus on poor children, and proportionately few of these children go to private schools under the current system. Thus, with a targeted voucher plan, the existing private school kids represent a small financial burden that can easily be overcome by the savings that occur as public kids go private. Still, the right structural choices must be made to ensure desired budgetary outcomes. Designers must determine the proper size of the vouchers, and at what times and in what numbers existing private school students will become eligible for vouchers.

this is counterproductive, because it essentially rewards schools for losing kids, and thus rewards them for poor performance and lack of responsiveness—but again, the critics of markets don't see it this way. They think improvement can only come with additional resources, and they want to see the public schools have as much funding as possible. In practice, that means making the vouchers much smaller than the average per-child expenditure in the public system, and holding the rest of the money back for the public schools—giving them more than would be justified on the basis of fixed costs alone.

The Milwaukee voucher system is a good example of such an arrangement. The basic rule, complications aside, is that only half of the full government funding goes with the child attending private school, and the other half stays with the Milwaukee public schools. With average spending per child at about $10,000 per year in that district, this means that a voucher of about $5,000 goes to pay for the child's education at a participating private school, and the remaining $5,000 stays with the district—for work it doesn't have to do. Not a bad deal, and hardly a drain on district finances.[23]

IS THERE A BEST STRUCTURE?

These are just some of the options that come into play, or could, when a choice system is being designed. Even from this brief discussion, however, it should be clear that a voucher system may in fact bear little resemblance to a free market—and may rather easily, through the conscious choice of rules, be designed to meet the needs of disadvantaged kids, to promote fairness and social equity, and to protect the public schools from unwarranted harm. There are many permutations, many possible designs.

---

[23]For a detailed discussion of the Milwaukee voucher plan, see John F. Witte, *The Market Approach to Education: An Analysis of America's First Voucher Program* (Princeton, N.J.: Princeton University Press, 2000).

But what kind of choice system is best? This is a question that has no objective answer. In the first place, different people may give priority to different social values, and thus have entirely different interpretations of what it means for a choice system to work to social advantage. Some may put greatest emphasis on personal freedom and student achievement, others on social equity, still others on promoting good citizenship—and these differences cannot be settled scientifically. We can't say that some values are better than others, that some people are right and others wrong.

Even if people could agree on the values to be pursued, moreover, they may still have very different expectations about what will actually happen when a choice system is designed in one way rather than another. Will Structure A lead to better student performance? Will Structure B promote balkanization along religious or racial lines? Which one will create better opportunities for disadvantaged kids? These are essentially questions about cause and effect—questions that, at least in principle, do have objective answers. But the problem is that, given the current state of social science theory and research, we often do not know exactly what the answers are, and there is plenty of room for legitimate debate.

For both these reasons, then—different values, different assessments of cause and effect—there will inevitably be disagreement over what a desirable choice system ought to look like. This is quite normal, though, and the same could be said for almost any type of public policy. Precisely because there are so many aspects of structure that go into the design of a choice system, moreover, and thus so many permutations that can be mixed and matched, there are tremendous possibilities for compromise among decision makers who are well intentioned and dedicated to finding a workable solution that is satisfactory—if not best—for almost everyone. A free-market supporter may prefer a universal voucher system with no restrictions on private schools but may be willing to accept a small pilot program that targets needy kids and imposes certain regulations. A liberal who is suspicious of unregulated choice may be willing to accept such a program as well, seeing it as a way of promoting social equity while protecting against the uncertainties of the free market.

A targeted system is not, of course, the only compromise that might work. What the availability of multiple designs really does, more generally, is to allow communities to build whatever kinds of choice systems seem to make the most sense for them, given their own unique mixtures of values and expectations, and their own ways of hammering out compromises and making political decisions. There can be as many different choice systems as there are communities.

THE POLITICS OF STRUCTURAL CHOICE

I should emphasize, once again, that the point of all this is to use the power of markets to the benefit of society, and thus to inject new options, stronger incentives, greater dynamism— and more equity—into a heavily bureaucratic education system that has long done almost nothing to take advantage of what choice and competition have to offer. There are many ways to do this and many designs on which reasonable people might agree. But it is important to keep this fundamental goal in mind, because some designs are better at achieving it than others, and some can be so restrictive that they prevent choice and competition from working at all.

Designers need to recognize any trade-offs they are making. They may have legitimate concerns about equity, democratic accountability, public school finances, and other matters, and they may design structures that protect and promote such values. That is an essential part of their job. But if these structures get too burdensome or are overly constraining—for example, in restricting the supply of private schools, or imposing costly and complex regulations, or keeping the size of the voucher very small—then much of the power of choice and competition may be lost in the process. The challenge is to strike the right balance—to unleash what choice and competition can contribute, but to channel them in socially desirable directions.

In principle, this is a straightforward objective that well-intentioned designers could readily pursue. In practice, however, the design of a choice system is an exercise in the making of public policy, and virtually every decision is determined through the political process—which is heavily shaped by power and self-interest. All too often, the very nature of politics makes it difficult for communities (and states and the nation as a whole) to design and adopt choice systems that work as well as they could.[24]

This kind of problem afflicts many areas of public policy, but it is especially acute in education because of the extraordinary political power of the teachers unions. The teachers unions have a strong self-interest in preserving the purely governmental system of top-down control that has prevailed since the Progressive Era. This is a system that works to their great advantage. By keeping the system as it is, they are guaranteed a safe, noncompetitive environment in which to organize teachers and engage in collective bargaining, and they are assured of substantial levels of membership and resources. And precisely because these foundations are secure, and because their deep pockets and huge memberships readily translate into tremendous political clout with elected officials, they are assured of having massive influence at all levels of the system.[25]

---

[24]See Moe, "The Politics of Bureaucratic Structure"; David Mayhew, *Congress: The Electoral Connection* (New Haven, Conn.: Yale University Press, 1974); and Mathew D. McCubbins, Roger G. Noll, and Barry R. Weingast, "Administrative Procedures as Instruments of Political Control," *Journal of Law, Economics, and Organization* 3 (1984): 243–77.

[25]For a more detailed discussion of the political power and organizational interests of the teachers unions, and the role the unions have played in the politics of school choice, see Terry M. Moe, "Teachers Unions and the Public Schools," in Moe, *A Primer on America's Schools*. See also Myron Lieberman, *The Teacher Unions* (New York: Free Press, 1997).

School choice, and especially vouchers, would change all this. A voucher system would allow money and children to flow from public to private, threatening a sharp drop in union membership and resources. It would disperse teachers to private schools, where they would be much harder for unions to organize. It would promote competition among schools, which would put union schools at a disadvantage (because of their higher costs and organizational rigidities). And it would create a more decentralized, less regulated system in which the unions would have less power and control.

Not surprisingly, the teachers unions are totally opposed to vouchers. This opposition arises because vouchers threaten their fundamental interests as organizations, and has little to do with how vouchers affect the opportunities of children, the quality of the schools, social equity, democracy, or any other basic social values. If it could be shown with 100 percent certainty that vouchers are good for kids, good for schools, and good for social equity and democracy, the unions would still be opposed to them. Indeed, they are even stridently opposed to vouchers that are only available to the poorest children in the worst public schools.

It would be nice to think that, with a choice system giving policymakers such a vast range of options, well-intentioned decision makers would find many ways of using choice and competition to improve upon the existing top-down system. The reality of politics, however, is that the teachers unions are by far the most powerful actors in the world of education policy, and they employ their power with a vengeance to protect the existing system, and to prevent vouchers and other types of choice systems from being adopted at all. Moreover, when they don't have quite enough power to stop some version of choice from being adopted, they use what power they have to insist on structural designs that minimize the amount of choice and competition the system will actually deliver—and to turn the program, if they can, into an empty shell that doesn't threaten their interests.

The upshot is that serious, thoroughgoing proposals for school choice are usually defeated in American politics. And those that succeed in getting adopted—the real-world choice systems now in operation—are often burdened with structures that do not put choice and competition to fully effective use in promoting important social values, and indeed are intended to stifle their impacts.

Consider, for example, the original design of the Milwaukee voucher program. In this first breakthrough for the voucher movement, the unions and their allies weren't able to stop a choice system from being adopted for low-income kids in Milwaukee. But they did succeed in (among other things) restricting eligibility to just 1,000 kids in a district of 100,000, prohibiting vouchers for religious schools, and prohibiting nonreligious schools from participating if more than half their kids would use vouchers. As a result, just seven schools initially signed up to be part of the program, and these schools did not have nearly enough slots to handle even the 1,000 kids who were eligible to receive vouchers. The number of kids exercising choice was thus kept quite low, to a mere 341 in the first year. And during the first six years of the program, these built-in limitations on the supply side led to a situation in which fully three-fourths of the voucher students attended just three private schools.[26]

Meantime, Milwaukee was being portrayed as a critical test of the efficacy of vouchers. For almost anyone with an interest in the issue, it seemed, evidence from the Milwaukee experience was awaited with bated breath, and was the subject of much publicity and controversy. But most of this hullabaloo was quite unnecessary and misplaced. The fact is, Milwaukee was not a critical test at all. The program gave vouchers to very few children. It allowed kids very few schools in the private sector to choose from. It provided the

---

[26]Again, see Witte, *The Market Approach to Education,* for details of the Milwaukee program.

public schools with almost no competition. And the question that mesmerized everyone's attention—whether kids actually learned more as a result of vouchers—was hardly worth exploring. What difference does it make if the kids in three private schools do or do not outperform the kids in the public schools? In this case, comparisons of student achievement could tell us little about what choice and competition are capable of contributing, because the enemies of the program did everything they could to see that there was as little choice and as little competition as possible.

The teachers unions and their allies have done the same in trying to limit other forms of school choice as well. Charter schools, for example, are public schools of choice that are granted substantial autonomy from district control and offer parents alternatives to the regular public schools. Unlike a voucher program, charter schools do not allow money and children to flow from public to private, but they are still threatening to union interests. They draw money and kids away from the regular public schools where union members teach, and their teachers need not be part of the district collective-bargaining contract. In attracting students away, moreover, the charters have an advantage because they are freer to design programs that appeal to parents, and they are less burdened by the costs and organizational rigidities of the regular schools. The greater the number of charter schools, therefore, the greater the threat to the size and financial well-being of the unions. And as charters spread, the unions and the districts will simply have less control over public education, and less power over the things that they care about.

As we ought to expect, the teachers unions have battled to prevent charters from succeeding. And when they have failed to stop the adoption of a charter plan—or when they have "supported" charters as a means of heading off vouchers (which they fear even more)—they have consistently pressured for structures that limit the program's scope and impact. Among other things, they lobby for low ceilings on the number of charters that can be created, for requirements that charter teachers be unionized and part of the district bargaining agreement, for low levels of funding, for no assistance with building or set-up costs, and for the extension of as many district regulations and controls as possible. Charters are on the rise nationwide. But due to the power of the unions and their allies, most are constrained by charter laws that sharply restrict how much choice and competition the new schools can really bring.[27]

Whether we look at voucher systems or charter systems, then, or indeed at any other real-world choice systems, the picture is not a pretty one. At least in this early phase of reform, with the established interests so powerful, there tends to be a yawning gap between how these new programs could perform, given the right design, and how they actually do perform.

What are we to make of this situation? As I mentioned earlier, economists tend to be unhappy with what politics does to the market economy, producing regulations that are too numerous, too burdensome, and sometimes counterproductive. Even so, they view our nation's imperfect economic system as far preferable to a centrally controlled economy in which markets play little or no role. And they use what political clout they have, mainly in the form of expert advice, to push for more rational and productive frameworks of economic regulation (which often involve substantial, but not total, deregulation).

We have to approach school choice in much the same way. Real-world choice systems are not built by well-intentioned designers who simply want to put choice and competition to their best possible social uses. They are products of politics,

---

[27]On charter schools and their politics, see Chester E. Finn Jr., Bruno V. Manno, and Gregg Vanourek, *Charter Schools in Action: Renewing Public Education* (Princeton, N.J.: Princeton University Press, 2000); Bryan Hassel, *The Charter School Challenge* (Washington, D.C.: Brookings Institution Press, 1999); and Hubert Morken and Jo Renee Formicola, *The Politics of School Choice* (Lanham, Md.: Rowman and Littlefield, 1999).

and are subject to influence by their political enemies—who want to them to be limited, and even to fail. Nonetheless, even these imperfect choice systems are preferable to a purely governmental system that makes no use of markets whatever. And as the choice movement grows in political power, which seems a good bet, these imperfections can be addressed over time through increasingly better designs that allow choice and competition to expand considerably and better realize their potential.

CONCLUSION

Whatever one's values may be, and even if one puts almost exclusive emphasis on social equity, it is difficult to argue that American education should not move toward a greater reliance on choice and competition. The system that we have now was designed in the early 1900s and has been frozen in time, a legacy of the past that traps "modern" education in an antiquated iron cage. As a form of organization, it is at the extreme end of the continuum: a system of top-down control by public officials and administrators that makes no serious attempt to take advantage of what choice and competition might have to offer. Eons ago, such an extreme form of organization might have seemed reasonable. But today there is a mountain of social science evidence demonstrating that market forces are powerful engines of efficiency, incentives, and social welfare. To make no use of them at all is simply a mistake.

It is also a mistake, however, to think that the only alternative to top-down government is the free market, in which the entire education system is privatized and schools and families are thrown into the marketplace to fend for themselves. Although public discussions of the choice issue (including academic research) have often been oriented by the logic and metaphor of the free market, the fact is that almost no one outside a small band of libertarians is actually calling for reforms that would shift American education all the way to the other end of the continuum. What choice advocates almost always have in mind, and what choice critics would be wise to consider (for their own social purposes), are forms of organization that lie in-between the extremes and involve important elements of both government and markets.

Because this is so, the most useful way to think of any system of school choice is not simply in terms of markets per se, but in terms of how much and what kinds of government they involve—and thus in terms of their structures. In the public debate over school choice, issues of structure are almost always ignored or given short shrift. But they are actually the key to the whole thing.

Two points are fundamental. The first is that there is always a structure to any choice system—a specific framework of basic governmental rules—and the details of this structure determine how choice and competition operate, how well the system performs, and what social values it promotes. One voucher system may make all children eligible, provide vouchers of equal value to all kids, allow parents to add on, and impose no rules of fairness or accountability on the private schools. Another voucher system may extend vouchers only to poor children in low-performing school districts, prevent parents from adding on, and require private schools to follow basic rules to ensure that students are treated equally and fairly, that curricula and teachers meet certain standards, that students are learning, and that money is properly handled. Both are choice systems—but knowing this, and this alone, tells us very little about what we can expect from them. Clearly, our expectations are very different from one system to the next. And the difference is due to structure.

The second point is that, just as there is a structure of choice, so there is a choice of structures. In between the extremes of pure governmental control and the free market, there are countless structures that might be adopted for any given choice system, and the people who are in a position to design the system have a great deal of flexibility in putting together combinations of structural features that give them the kind of system they want. How choice works, and toward what ends, is not something that simply happens as a result of the automatic functioning of the market. It is largely a matter of conscious design. When policymakers know what social values they want to achieve, they can choose the structural features that, by virtue of the specific ways they constrain and direct the power of choice and competition, best promote those values.

As things now stand, all of these advantages cannot be realized. Real-world choice systems are designed in the political process, and there are strong forces of self-interest and parochialism lobbying for structures that strictly limit what choice and competition can do. The designs that actually get adopted, as a result, are usually not what well-intentioned designers would prefer, and are but a pale reflection of what is possible. But they are at least a beginning, and represent important and necessary steps toward designs that put markets to effective social use in education. Further steps can only be taken as the choice movement grows in political power—and as the policymakers, who respond to power, make greater efforts to use choice and competition to social advantage.

In the meantime, it is important for people of good faith to see the choice issue in a less simplistic and more constructive light. The fact is that choice is a social force of tremendous power, but how that power is used—which values it promotes and how well it promotes them—depends entirely on the structures in which it is embedded, structures that we as a society are able to choose. The challenge for American education at this juncture in history is to get beyond ideological battles over markets versus government, and instead to think pragmatically about markets *and* government—and how both can be used, in strategic combination, to yield the results we want for our children and our society.

Contributors

DAVID E. CAMPBELL is an assistant professor in the Department of Political Science at the University of Notre Dame.

JOHN E. CHUBB is chief education officer and one of the founders of Edison Schools Inc, a private manager of public schools, including many charter schools. Edison Schools today operates 136 schools in twenty-two states and the District of Columbia, serving some 75,000 students. He is the co-author (with Terry M. Moe) of *Politics, Markets, and America's Schools*, a seminal work that argues for the introduction of free-market principles within the American educational system.

KACEY GUIN is a graduate student at the Daniel J. Evans School of Public Affairs at the University of Washington and a research assistant in the Evans School's Center on Re-Inventing Public Education.

ERIC A. HANUSHEK is the Paul and Jean Hanna Senior Fellow at the Hoover Institution. His works on education policy include *Improving America's Schools: The Role of Incentives; Making*

Schools Work: Improving Performance and Controlling Costs; and *Educational Performance of the Poor: Lessons from Rural Northeast Brazil*. His current research involves understanding the role of teachers, programs, and funding in determining student achievement.

PAUL T. HILL is a research professor in the Daniel F. Evans School of Public Affairs and director of the Center on Reinventing Public Education, both at the University of Washington. The center develops and helps communities adopt alternative governance systems for public K–12 education. His most recent publication (with R. J. Lake) is *Charter Schools and Accountability in Public Education*.

CAROLINE M. HOXBY, Distinguished Visiting Fellow at the Hoover Institution, is a professor of economics at Harvard University. She is the editor of the recently published book, *The Economic Analysis of School Choice*, and the author of numerous influential papers on education policy, including "Does Competition Among Public Schools Benefit Students and Taxpayers?"

TERRY M. MOE, senior fellow at the Hoover Institution and professor of political science at Stanford University, is the author of *Schools, Vouchers, and the American Public*, and the co-author (with John E. Chubb) of *Politics, Markets, and America's Schools*. He also edited *Private Vouchers* and *A Primer on America's Schools*.

PAUL E. PETERSON is a senior fellow at the Hoover Institution and the Henry Lee Shattuck Professor of Economics at Harvard University and director of the Program on Education Policy and Governance at Harvard University. He is the editor in chief of *Education Next* and the author of several important works on U.S. education, including *Earning and Learning; How Schools Matter; Learning from School*

Choice; The Politics of School Reform: 1870–1940; and *School Politics Chicago Style.*

MARTIN R. WEST is a graduate student in the Department of Government at Harvard University and a research associate in Harvard's Program on Education Policy and Governance.

Index